What others say . . .

Whoever receives the message of this book will have a new and vital understanding of what biblical faith is all about. More than that, the reader will be wonderfully encouraged to step out in such faith and to make a difference for the Kingdom. Bob, I know, lives out that faith in his healing ministry, which is blessing so many.

This book will rock your faith and set you ablaze with world-impact faith. Your shadow will become dangerous. It's lethal. Shake off doubt and unbelief and take the plunge into a life of Kingdom advancement.

Pastor C. John Dekker, Northland, New Zealand

This book captures much of the wisdom and insights underlying the ministry and healing which you see demonstrated and lived out in Bob's life and ministry. It is a treasure chest of truth and wisdom to give depth to those of us who are learning to step out in faith and to develop our spiritual gifts and ministry to greater depths of anointing and effectiveness.

Franklyn Elliott, Senior Pastor, Metro North Christian Centre, National Adviser for the National Association of Healing Rooms Australia

As a family doctor I am interested in healing for my patients – spirit, mind and body. During Bob's visits to my medical clinic we have seen Jesus do real miracles – instant healing of emphysema, arthritis, fractures and lots more! Read this book. You will be as blessed as I was. Jesus wants to do beautiful things to your insides!

Dr. Louise Holliday, Sydney, Australia

God is raising up a people filled with faith and righteous empowerment in the midst of a world plagued by negativity, unbelief and skepticism. Bob Brasset's book, *All Things Are Possible*, will truly refresh, revitalize, and power you up in this critical hour.

Patricia King, Extreme Prophetic Ministry Kelowna, BC, Canada

This text presents issues of faith, abiding in Jesus, etc. in practical terms for believers. You'll find no pat answers here. Instead, Bob Brasset presents a compelling and practical vision of the Kingdom of God – a living, daily walk with Jesus. New and mature believers will be encouraged and challenged by this book. It is a must-read for those wanting to understand significant issues of Christian character, maturity, and power.

The Reverend Dr. John Roddam
Rector: St. Luke's, Seattle, Washington

I have had the privilege of knowing Bob and Sue Brasset for over fifteen years. Little did I know the impact God would have on my life through them. Over the last five years Bob has truly been a father and a mentor to me. My life and ministry were transformed by "the love anointing", and I was launched into a healing ministry as well.

One of the subjects Bob and I talked about many times was true believing. It seemed that the kind of faith many Christians exhibited was actually a type of "make believe". They were trying to create what they imagined by sheer will power. Often in his meetings Bob would focus on the keys of anointed believing. Since those early discussions I've heard this message develop into the message of this book. I highly recommend this book to those who want to live in the realm of anointed believing, with a faith that wins battles from a place of rest.

Terry Somerville
Miracles In The Marketplace television program
Total Change Ministries, British Columbia

In *All Things Are Possible*, Bob Brasset is a savvy spiritual scout leading us through the wilderness of Western Church unbelief and the minefields of untried truth into a supernatural resting place of insight that is simple yet profound, mysterious and yet practical. His poignant perspectives, stirring examples, and inspiring testimonies are exactly what the Church today needs to hear. Few books I have read in recent years articulate the true nature of faith and the keys of the Kingdom of God with the kind of revelatory wisdom that Bob Brasset offers as a practitioner, not a theoretician. I highly recommend it to anyone who wants to be challenged to another level of living in the compassion and power of Jesus in daily life.

Don Toshach
Free to Fly Ministries, San Diego, CA

If you want a boost of encouragement in the arena of divine healing, this book is a must read for anyone wanting to get a heavenly perspective of real faith and the gift of healing.

I have ministered with Bob and have watched him minister in action, and he walks out a model that so much reflects the content of his teaching in this book. Bob's childlike faith and trust in God, allows him to break through into heaven and then God invades his meetings.

Gord and Jan Whyte
Co-Leaders: New Life Church Kelowna B.C. Canada
Founders: Healing Gate Ministries International

All Things Are Possible

The Power of Anointed Believing

Bob Brasset

Sovereign World

Sovereign World Ltd
PO Box 777
Tonbridge
Kent TN11 0ZS
England

ISBN 1 85240 425 6

Cover design by CCD, www.ccdgroup.co.uk
Typeset by CRB Associates, Reepham, Norfolk
Printed in the United States of America

Contents

Dedication

- To my wife Sue: friend, helper and committed partner on our pilgrimage in healing the sick in the authority of Jesus.
- To Jimmy Brasset, my brother, and his wife Lynda, who have given many hours of diligent labor contributing much to the completion of this book.
- To my sons, Bill, Paul and Chris, and to my daughter Heather, who encouraged me all along the way.

Foreword

by John Arnott

As long as I have known Bob Brasset, he has been a man hard after God. He is particularly moved and motivated to see powerful book of Acts type healings restored to the Church and available to God's people. Bob has invested years to bring outstanding physical miracles to hundreds of people, yet ever-learning all the way. His new book will help you receive faith for miracles. A faith that is rooted and grounded in love. A faith that rests in the finished work of Christ. It is a faith that will enable and equip you also to to be a carrier and a bringer of the Kingdom of God with signs, miracles and wonders.

John Arnott
Senior pastor, Toronto Airport Christian Fellowship
and Catch the Fire Ministries

Foreword

by Todd Bentley

Bob Brasset's teaching in this book presents some of the most anointed insights on walking in the faith of the Bible that I've heard. The material in this book issues a clarion call to advance God's Kingdom.

Bob has a true healing/miracle anointing for the nations. In this book he issues the challenge for others to walk in the same healing/miracle anointing. If you want to cultivate Kingdom faith and become a Kingdom advancer like he is, then this book is a must read.

Radical lovers of God truly hunger to experience a faith that is not sterile and cold but a faith that is anointed by love. In this book Bob not only leads us into such a faith but also into a glorious participation of the divine nature. He masterfully demonstrates that becoming co-laborers with our divine Lord is our divine destiny. Bob's book will be an inspiring guide.

Todd Bentley
Evangelist/Revivalist
Founder of Fresh Fire Ministries

Chapter 1

Believe and Make-Believe

"Only believe," Smith Wigglesworth used to say repeatedly in his meetings. I struggled with that. It seemed the more I believed with my mind, my thoughts, and my strong desire, the less I saw. Then, one day, I discovered that there is a vast difference between *mentally believing* (or comprehending) something and *believing with our hearts*. This believing with our hearts, or heart-felt faith, I now call "anointed believing".

Believing? That means faith, doesn't it? But what is faith? How does it come to us? How does it operate? Does it make things real? Is faith a matter of squeezing your eyes shut tight, wrinkling your brow, puckering your lips and believing with all your might that there really is a tooth fairy? Of course not! No matter how hard you try to make it happen and no matter how much you concentrate, the tooth fairy will never pop into existence. Peter Pan will never fly around your bedroom ceiling. The Easter Bunny will never hop out from the laundry hamper. And Santa Clause won't be dropping down your chimney this Christmas. Not in Virginia. Not in Kansas. Not anywhere.

God, on the other hand, is real. Whether you believe it or not; whether you have faith in Him or not; whether you acknowledge Him or not. If you follow His commandments or break every law in the book; if you look for His footprints in the sand or signs in the sky, cry out to Him or curse His name, study His word or studiously ignore Him ... The I AM really is. And His existence and His Divine Character are not dependent one scintilla on how much you believe or don't believe.

Faith might be described as a bridge to the unseen, but not to the unreal. It isn't simply make believe. Faith is not a magical force that simply promotes or acquires our desires. It's not a metaphysical, mental, or emotionally-induced state conjured up to get that DVD player we'd like or a box of groceries we desperately need. In fact, it's not about our own efforts at all. It's another quality entirely. Faith, it says in God's word, is *"the substance of things hoped for, the evidence of things not seen"* (Hebrews 11:1). Four words sum up faith: *Faith comes from God.* Now, we're getting somewhere. When we talk about faith we start with God. Leave Him out and no matter how many symbols, numbers and figures you put on the left side of the equation, the right side will always equal zero.

Faith, then, flows out of:

- Knowing God
- Knowing His character more than His deeds (Psalm 103:7)
- Knowing what He wants in a particular situation
- Obeying what He shows you to act upon
- Trusting Him to do that which is impossible for you

Paul said to the Romans, *"Faith comes by hearing, and hearing by the word of God"* (Romans 10:17). For years we have taken this passage from Romans to mean, "If you keep hearing the word, faith will come." There was a time when I believed and taught this passage that way. That, however, is not what this passage from Romans is saying. History and experience do not confirm that interpretation. Neither does the context.

If just hearing the word would build faith, why aren't all those who quote, study, memorize and confess the word working miracles, healing the sick and raising the dead? To understand this, or any other scripture, we must understand it in the light of its context, which is the previous ten chapters of Romans about faith, righteousness and the new birth experience. Faith for salvation (the new birth) does indeed come by hearing the word. The scripture asks *"how shall they hear without a preacher?"* (verse 14).

On the other hand, faith for healing, faith for miracles comes not just from hearing the word (Christ is the healer) but from intimacy and trust in the Healer – Jesus! Faith is founded upon hearing Christ – His word specifically for you – and then, on the basis of that word and His trustworthiness, launching out in obedience.

Scriptural faith is not declaring some ridiculous or arbitrary thing and then expecting it to happen. That is at best, presumption. And yet it sometimes passes for genuine Bible faith. But biblical faith is active. It anticipates the answer and the blessing.

I find that when I believe and when Jesus' anointing follows, something powerful happens. Miracles occur; people get healed; signs and wonders flow. It is quite exhilarating. In fact, it's the only way I want to live the rest of my life. I want Jesus' anointing to permeate every aspect of my faith in Him, every aspect of my willingness to trust Him, every aspect of my life. A day without miracles is a boring day! I don't even want to have "divine appointments" any more. I want to *be* a living, walking, breathing divine appointment.

Divine appointment at 34,000 feet

It was to be six days of teaching, equipping, healing and impartation and Sue and I were to thoroughly enjoy our time at Toronto Airport Christian Fellowship in June of 2003.

The healings actually began on our plane trip there, as the jet became a healing room. About two hours into our flight from Victoria, B.C., to Toronto a voice came over the P.A., "Is there a doctor present on the flight? We have a medical emergency."

After 20 minutes or so I stood up to go to the rest room. Sue said, "Find out if you can, what the medical emergency is." As I proceeded toward the rear of the plane, I noticed an elderly lady quietly weeping. I leaned over.

"Excuse me," I said, "but I am a minister. Was it your husband who had the medical emergency?"

She replied, "Yes. The doctor thinks it's a stroke and my husband also has Alzheimer's."

I asked her if I could pray with her. "Oh, yes, please," she agreed. I sat down next to her. She told me that he had also had a sudden worsening of his Alzheimer's, and then what appeared to be the stroke. She told me that although her husband had been a pastor for over 40 years, she didn't particularly believe in healing.

"That's okay," I assured her, "I have enough faith for us both. Let's pray." I then spoke blessing and healing and rebuked the cause and effect of Alzheimer's and of a cerebral vascular incident. At the very moment I said, "Amen," the flight attendant came.

"Excuse me, ma'am, I have good news," she said. "Just moments ago, your husband suddenly returned to normal. The doctor doesn't understand it, but he seems to be just fine!" The woman expressed great joy and thankfulness and then told me, "My stomach pain is gone! I think I'm healed, also! I'll have my breakfast, now – I couldn't eat it earlier."

Upon returning to my seat, I was asked by the man sitting next to me what had happened. I told him about the healing of the husband and wife. "Well, I'm not a Christian," he responded. "In fact, I've never been in a church in my entire life. But I have severe migraine headaches. Do you think God would heal me if you prayed?" I told him, yes. He went on to tell me that the headaches were triggered by cheese, chocolate or red wine. When I finished praying, my wife Sue leaned over and, not knowing of the prayer or my companion's medical condition, asked if I would like a chocolate. She then offered one to the gentleman, as well. "Okay," he said, "I'm willing to test out if I'm healed. I'll eat the chocolate." He did so and experienced no problem or pain throughout the remainder of the flight. Later, Sue and I also had an opportunity to pray with the flight attendant.

Hidden dangers

I'm convinced that mental "believism" is a counterfeit and is present in our church activities and even in some of our healing services. In fact, it's toxic. It does much damage and even seeks to infect and harm those who have true faith.

There is a story of one family with a child who had diabetes. The parents prayed for their girl for her healing. They read the Scriptures and became convinced of God's willingness to heal their daughter. They saw the necessity of stepping out in faith. They felt that since God had done His part, they must do theirs. Reading and quoting healing Scriptures constantly, they convinced themselves mentally. They prayed, fasted and pressed in vigorously. Their next step, because they felt that Jesus provided for full healing 2,000 years ago on the cross, was to "step out" and to refuse all life-saving insulin injections for their child.

The child got worse. They persevered in their "faith" and faith confessions. Several days later, the child died. What a tragedy! After many months of depression, the family began to be restored. "We were never more convinced that our daughter was healed," they said, "than just before she died."

What went wrong?

My feeling is that, for this dear, well-meaning family, mental believism had turned to presumption. The chart on p. 14 presents what I consider is the contrast between toxic faith and anointed faith, or mental believism and anointed believing.

Allow me at this point, to give several definitions that embody faith:

1. *Trust*. The Greek word translated "faith" is probably more accurately translated "trust". Exercising faith means that you are putting your trust in the completely-trustworthy One.
2. *An inward response to a faithful person*. Faith is always a response to a person, never to a process. It is never just believing a principle or an impersonal "word". Even the Scriptures are dead and impersonal without the Spirit's anointing. *"God ... made us ... ministers of the new covenant, not of the letter, but of the Spirit; for the letter kills, but the Spirit gives life"* (2 Corinthians 3:6). This means that we need the prompting and the anointing of the Holy Spirit on all that we believe and do. Otherwise, we can bring forth only death, not life.
3. *Jesus*. Most Christians realize that Jesus is the Author of our faith – that is, He is the One who gave us the faith we now possess. He gave us the free gift of faith and it was enough faith for us to be saved. This is a wonderful thing. But how many of us realize that Jesus is also the Finisher of our faith? (Hebrews 12:2) That means that He also brings it to completion. *"He who has begun a good work in you will complete it until the day of Jesus Christ"* (Philippians 1:6). The good work

Toxic faith (mental believism)	True faith (anointed believing)
Make-believe – takes place through programming our own thoughts	*"What really matters is . . . faith expressed in love"* (Galatians 5:6, *The Message*)
You control it with your mind	Spirit empowered. *"Jesus* [is] *the author and finisher of our faith"* (Hebrews 12:2)
Pharisees and religious leaders had this and were admonished for it, e.g., *"Faith by itself, if it does not have works, is dead"* (James 2:17) *"You search the Scriptures, for in them you think you have eternal life . . . "* (John 5:39)	Roman centurion had this kind of faith (see Matthew, chapter 8)
James said this kind of false faith and the wisdom that comes from it is *"earthly, sensual, demonic"* (James 3:15)	*". . .* [is] *expressed in love"* (Galatians 5:6, *The Message*)
Characterized by boasting, e.g., "I have all the faith in the world"	*"Lord, I believe; help my unbelief"* (Mark 9:24)
Lacks intimacy because it's mechanical and impersonal	Full of intimacy, trust, warmth
Haughty, arrogant, intolerant and critical of others who don't have *their* kind of faith	Meek, lowly and humble
Can sometimes even do great exploits, i.e., "move mountains", but is like a *"sounding brass or a clanging cymbal"* (1 Corinthians 13:1)	Can transform hearts and bears fruit that will remain (John 15:5)
Self-centred, materialistic	Selfless, directed towards others and eternal realities

He began in us was the "new birth" experience. It was the beginning stage of our faith-walk with Jesus. Now, if we will depend on Him day by day, He will build our faith and bring it to completion at the second coming. What a wonderful thought. What wonderful things we can anticipate as we continually trust in Him.

4. *Taking God seriously*. God takes His own words very seriously. We need to as well. So many Christians claim to have faith but don't take God seriously. Derek Prince says, "To take God seriously means to take His word and His desire to communicate seriously. If a person speaks to us but we ignore or even reject much of what they say to us, we are certainly not taking that person seriously. In fact, we are disrespecting that person."[1]

The same applies to God. We must listen to all He says. And not just listen, but listen seriously, with a heart to obey.

5. *Faith is the substantial power by which a thing desired becomes a thing possessed*. It is substantial, being the substance of things hoped for, the evidence of things not seen. Yet in spite of its great power, faith remains intangible. It can't be weighed or measured – not by us at least. That would be like attempting to define "energy" in a single sentence. Impossible. Jesus said that it was like a mustard seed in Matthew 17:20, *"I tell you the truth, if you have faith as small as a mustard seed, you can say to this mountain, 'Move from here to there' and it will move. Nothing will be impossible for you"* (NIV). Notice that Jesus did not emphasize how much faith it took to do great things. Rather He emphasized how *little* faith it took to do great things.

Tom Gliebe is an associate minister with Todd Bentley's Fresh Fire Ministries. He makes some interesting and, I feel, helpful comments about the substance of faith. Here is what he said in a recent newsletter:

Recently an incident took place that gave me great insight into faith, its operations and its function. It was one of those normal days at the ministry office when we were blessed by a surprise visit from Charlie Robinson and his son, Gabriel. Charlie is on staff and ministers with Todd Bentley of Fresh Fire Ministries. They had just returned from ministering with Todd in several different nations. They were very excited as they told us about the many miracles they had seen in several countries and began sharing about one particular outstanding miracle that happened in Africa. It was concerning a man who only had sight in one eye and was not only blind in the other, but only had an empty socket where the other eye should have been. In spite of the fact that there was, "... nothing to work with", they had seen so many outstanding miracles that they were full of faith, so that they put their hands over the empty socket and prayed that God would "give him a new eye!" After praying, they covered the man's good eye, held up three fingers and asked him how many fingers they were holding up. Even though nothing appeared to have changed in the natural, the man answered, "three." They did this several times and he continued to accurately tell them how many fingers they were holding up. Over the course of the next three days the eye formed and was complete! They were almost like little kids telling this remarkable story to us that they saw with their own eyes.

As they shared this amazing story with me something remarkable happened. I saw in a vision the man's eye formed in his empty socket before it was visible. The Lord had opened my eyes and revealed "faith in action"! What I saw was a "form" of an eye, like the structure of a house before the roof or walls are put on. The scripture in Genesis 1:2 came to mind that says, *"the earth was without form, and void; and darkness was on the face of the deep. And the Spirit of God was hovering over the face of the waters."* I immediately knew that "faith was a substance". It was the structure of the frame of the eye and I was seeing it! What God was revealing to me was that when a person is experiencing true faith something wonderful happens. In faith and by faith, he speaks and God creates. In this case, their prayer in faith caused the creative power to flow by the Spirit and "form" the framework of the eye. What I saw was the formation of the structure of the eye before the flesh had filled up the "form" created by faith! This was why the man could see (by faith)!

If any of you have ever worked in a metal shop you would know that in order to create anything, a plate, a statue, or a cup, one must first make a "form". In high school I took metal shop and will always remember how you would take two identical half boxes hinged together, fill them with a sand-like material, and place an object into it, such as a ball. They would then clamp the two forms together lightly, open them up, take out the ball and find two half holes that when placed together contained a perfect imprint of the ball. Clamping the form box together, the worker would then pour a material, whether plastic or metal, down a pour spout, which filled the hole inside the form. When it cooled and was opened one would find a new ball created in the structure of the emptiness of the form. This is what God showed me. I literally saw the form of a new eye created by faith in the void of his socket and made out of faith, which is a substance! During the ensuing three days of this African miracle, the flesh filled this form of faith and the eye was made visible. *"And the Word became flesh . . . "* (John 1:14).

By faith, the entire universe hangs on the structure or frame created by the Word of God. *"All things were made through Him, and without Him nothing was made that was made"* (John 1:3). It is truly amazing yet apparent that God created the Heavens and the earth by simply speaking in faith that which He called into being. Hebrews 11:3 says, *"By faith we understand that the worlds were framed by the word of God, so that the things which are seen were not made of things which are visible."* Now we, being Christian beings, need to operate in the image of our Father, duplicate the works of Jesus, do what the Father does and create life in ALL its facets, physical, emotional and spiritual.[2]

Notes

1. Prince, Derek, *Derek Prince Newsletter*, Florida: DP Ministries.
2. Gliebe, Tom, *Fire Gate Ministries*, PO Box 1000, Battle Ground, WA 98604.

Chapter 2

The Essence of Simplicity

"And a little child shall lead them."
(Isaiah 11:6)

Faith need not be any more complicated than a child's trust in and expectation of its parents. Little children are humble, and humility is the atmosphere God moves in. Just as water flows to the lowest level, so too the Holy Spirit (whom Jesus likened to water in John 7:38) seeks out the lowest or most basic level of humility. Children don't consider their parents' limitations or lack of resources when they make a request from them. They simply ask and expect. They trust.

Often in public meetings my wife Sue and I like to call a child forward. Perhaps the child will be six or seven years of age. In a gentle manner I ask the child if they would like to heal someone. I assure them it will be simple and that I will be there to help them, but not just me, most importantly Jesus is there to do the healing through them. Time after time we watch people weep and sob as they experience Jesus heal people through the simple command of a little child.

I think adults are often much too sophisticated. We complicate matters way beyond any necessity. Here's the way Paul put it, *"But I fear, lest somehow, as the serpent deceived Eve by his craftiness, so your minds may be corrupted from the simplicity that is in Christ"* (2 Corinthians 11:3). Many times we mistakenly strive for information when in reality, what we need is revelation. There is simplicity in Christ. There is a simplicity to the Gospel.

Simplicity, not simple-mindedness

Simplicity in Christ is not *simple-mindedness*. Rather, it is profound. And yet it is simple enough for a child to understand. God never speaks in confusion or uses vain, empty words. In fact, one way of knowing it is God speaking is that the answer is simple.

Jesus took complicated problems like blindness, paralysis and leprosy and delivered the answer in simple acts of obedience:

- Go wash (John 9:7)
- Rise up and walk (John 5:8)
- Go show yourself to the priest (Luke 17:14)
- Stretch out your hand (Matthew 12:13)

Pretty basic instructions, I'd say. Sophistication and analysis don't go far in understanding the dimensions of the Spirit. We can understand why Paul said,

> *"I came to you in weakness and fear, and with much trembling. My message and my preaching were not with wise and persuasive words, but with a demonstration of the Spirit's power."*
>
> (1 Corinthians 2:3–4 NIV).

Jesus rejoiced over this principle.

> *"I thank You, Father, Lord of heaven and earth, that You have hidden these things from the wise and prudent and revealed them to babes. Even so, Father, for so it seemed good in Your sight."*
>
> (Luke 10:21)

The attitude's the thing

Jesus exhibited a constant childlike dependence on His Father. In fact, He said, "I do those things I see my Father doing" (John 5:19); and later on, "I only say those things my Father has taught me" (John 8:28). One day His disciples were arguing about who was the greatest in the Kingdom. Jesus called a little child to Him and said, *"Anyone who will not receive the kingdom of God like a little child will never enter it"* (Mark 10:15 NIV).

In my own life, I have found it necessary to repent, to change my mind. I had to become like a little child before I could even "see" this supernatural dimension of healing, miracles, signs and wonders. As I develop and maintain a childlike delight and trust in the goodness of my heavenly Father, something happens. The heavens open up. The supernatural flows.

My little grandchildren squeal with delight when I play with them. They trust me. They aren't anxious, worried, fearful or concerned about impressing me. I find that worry, fear, anxiety and any attempt to impress people undercuts the anointing. Joy, a relaxed attitude, and childlike trust increases the anointing.

Lip service versus "life" service

All the above having been said, I still find it easier to pay lip service to this attitude of simple trust that Jesus talked about, than to actually live it. For me (and I suspect for many others) this is not achieved once for all time. It is a battleground! This might sound like a contradiction, but is in fact scriptural! Just as we must labor to enter His rest (Hebrews 4:11), we must labor or struggle to maintain that childlike attitude of trust.

When testing comes into our lives, when pressures and complications arise, we strive to analyze, to resolve, to rid ourselves of these problems. But as we search for complex solutions to these complicated problems, our attitude is not to be one of tension, fear and dismay. The very opposite is required.

For me personally, when a testing times comes, I find it imperative to take a deep breath (or perhaps a few of them), settle my spirit and re-establish or return to that basic, loving childlike faith and trust in the goodness of my heavenly Father. Not only is this effective, but this kind of attitude adjustment is immensely pleasing to God.

With or without faith

The Bible says, *"Without faith, it is impossible to please God"* (Hebrews 11:6 NIV). The opposite of this is also true. *With faith* it is impossible *not* to please God. This means that God's children, as they trust Him, are very pleasing to Him ... constantly. They bring great pleasure to His heart. In fact, it's the only way to bring pleasure to our Father. Works, striving, self-effort – none of these is pleasing. Any advancement in the Christian life is always by faith. Every expression of love, every work of charity, all of these must be mixed with faith in order to be pleasing to our Father. And yet it's not a burdensome thing. It is a very easy thing for a child of God to exercise faith because it is our new nature. We are *believers*.

The divine exchange

Because our Father takes so much pleasure in us, because we are family, because we are joint-heirs with Jesus, it is possible for Christians to enjoy total favor with our Father. It is not 90% or 98% favor, but 100% favor. This favor comes provided we believe it, receive it and walk in it. Jesus took our place in punishment for our sin so that we could take His place in favor with the Father. We've swapped a place of sin and condemnation for a place of favor with the Most High God. Pretty good deal?

Can you imagine how much the Father favors Jesus? Can you imagine how precious the Only Begotten Son is to the Father? How much love and constant favor the Father showers down on Jesus? That is the exact, precise amount of favor we can walk in for the rest of our lives, if we will receive it and walk in it each and every day. That's the secret of walking in miracles and experiencing heaven on earth. It is the exchanged life.

Jesus came to earth as our kinsman-redeemer. In taking our nature He became a true descendant of Adam. On the cross the entire evil inheritance of Adam – all the sin, all the rebellion, all the filth, came upon Jesus. Isaiah 53:6 says, *"The LORD has laid on Him the iniquity of us all."* This means that on the cross, Jesus took the evil that was due to us that we might receive the good and the favor that was His by eternal right. The cross was God's amazing divine exchange. It's an amazing deal!

The exchange

Jesus took away	We receive
Punishment for our sins	Peace, reconciliation and complete forgiveness
Sickness, infirmity, and illness	Healing, divine health
Guilt and sin	The righteousness of God
Curse and shame	Blessings of obedience
Poverty	His wealth
Death	Life in abundance (total favor)

We have an abundant provision for everything we need as it pertains to life and living a godly life.

> *"No temptation has overtaken you except such as is common to man; but God is faithful, who will not allow you to be tempted beyond what you are able, but with the temptation will also make the way of escape, that you may be able to bear it."*
>
> (1 Corinthians 10:13)

In the Kingdom of God through the provision of the redemptive work of Christ on the cross we enjoy absolute abundance. This means that we can never say, "There aren't enough healings or miracles." No, the Kingdom is brimming over with an enormous amount – more than we'll ever need – of all good things. We access all of these abundant provisions through anointed believing.

Imagine, if you will, a street beggar – a poor, emaciated, hungry and depressed wanderer. One cold and rainy night he's walking the streets when he passes a storefront. He looks in the window. Inside there is warmth and light and people and laughter and joy. It's an enormous banquet. Every imaginable kind of delicious, nutritious, succulent food is heaped high on the table. The guests are all partaking freely. He notices on the window a sign stating: "The Kingdom of God – Free Banquet".

Should he enter? Many in his circumstances would (and do) hesitate and turn away. The admission to this free banquet is anointed believing. This allows whosoever chooses to believe to enter in to that banquet and to live there. All the time.

Many Christians are living like that beggar – wandering aimlessly, cold, hungry and depressed. They don't realize that they have a right of access. The only requirement is that they believe it and receive it. It is absolute abundance and total favor.

Chapter 3

Questions and Answers

The Bible points to Abraham as an example of faith.

> *"And not being weak in faith, he did not consider his own body, already dead (since he was about a hundred years old), and the deadness of Sarah's womb."* (Romans 4:19)

The Greek word translated in this verse "not consider" is the word *katanao*. It can also be translated "to contemplate; to attentively consider; or to observe fully." The implication here is that Abraham fully considered two realities. Firstly, he considered his and Sarah's bodies. He knew that they were well past their child producing years. He didn't deny reality. He didn't grow strong in faith because he refused to acknowledge his natural circumstances. He simply saw another reality. In fact, he saw both dimensions – the natural and the spiritual. He had received revelation from God. That was a firm, spiritual reality for him.

Revelation is the superimposing of God's reality and God's plan on the circumstances of your life. It is the blueprint of God that shows you where you are going. When the Bible says that Abraham did not consider his own body, it's not telling us that he denied his body – that he turned a blind eye to its limitations and frailty. Instead, it is telling us that he did not consider the deadness of his own body, or his wife's body, as the final answer. Why? Because what this grand old man from Ur saw in the spirit (i.e. God's promise to him) was far more vivid and far more compelling than anything his natural eye could see. He saw a greater reality. One that didn't eliminate or ignore the other but encompassed and superseded it!

How did he do it? How could he be so sure of God's promise when that promise was so extraordinary? And how did he manage to continue for another 25 years, strong in his faith, sure of God's calling? He walked in and lived in the realm of God's own supernatural presence. Once we too, learn the secret, the discipline, of abiding in that realm, no delay will ever cause us to lose hope, and in God, nothing will be impossible. Abraham considered God's direct promise to him so *superior* to natural reality that it carried far more weight.

Faith gives us this insight into the unseen realm, revealing its tangible nature. This was certainly Paul's perspective.

> *"While we do not look at the things which are seen, but at the things which are not seen. For the things which are seen are temporary, but the things which are not seen are eternal."*
>
> (2 Corinthians 4:18)

Paul wasn't saying that we deny those things which are seen. He was saying that the things which are seen are only a small part of the equation. They're not, by themselves, the determining factor. God, in His eternal realm, has the final answer.

The principle is this: spirit controls matter. The spiritual realm is eternal, immortal, invisible, incorruptible and is infinitely more powerful than the natural realm. But this doesn't negate the natural realm. The natural or material realm is pretty real, too. Just try setting your hand down on a very hot stove for a minute. Or two. But it's only temporal. It's subject to decay, corruption and death. It's very much subservient to the spiritual, but it's still real.

My friend, Marc Brisbois, in writing on *Overcoming Deferred Hope*, in his April–June 2003 newsletter, said,

> "The greatest joy of having a promise is not the receiving of the thing promised. The greatest joy and reward of faith is its ability to take us above the plain of the natural. It enables us to transcend the fickle passions of human 'wants', to live in

the timeless presence of the Everlasting Father. The Words of Promise are not just I.O.U.'s we one day hope to collect on. Rather, they are windows into eternity. They give us the means to bask in the reality of the Lord's timeless dominion. With this resource in hand, maintaining one's confession of confidence is a simple task. No matter how long the wait."

Faith comes from hearing God

Eastern religions and mind-science cults tend to deny natural reality. They say that sickness, sin and disease are just illusions. That kind of thinking not only denies God's natural creation, it is counter to Scripture.

Christians too, sometimes make a similar mistake. They teach people to deny or ignore sickness. Acknowledging sickness or an impairment while trying to produce faith is considered to be walking in unbelief. Instead of denying natural circumstances, I encourage people to superimpose God's word to them personally over their very real natural circumstances. What God speaks is eternal, incorruptible and substantial. There is no limit to its power. The "title deed" to this massively abundant, eternal, supernatural realm is FAITH.

God visited Solomon in a dream and said, *"Ask! What shall I give you?"* (1 Kings 3:5). In verse 9, Solomon asked for *leb shome*.[1] This Hebrew word literally means, "a hearing heart". Isn't that amazing? I believe that's where all true wisdom comes from – a hearing heart – a heart that hears God, because God is the source of all true wisdom. Solomon didn't ask for a higher IQ or for great knowledge or practical understanding – things we might commonly associate with wisdom. Rather, he asked for a *hearing heart*. This is true scriptural wisdom. God's word goes forth continually, but true faith comes from hearing God.

Romans 10:17 says, *"Faith comes by hearing, and hearing by the word of God."* The NIV translation reads, *"... and ... is heard through the word of Christ."* In other words, faith comes when we hear God speaking to us. Abraham heard God speak to him. He had a hearing heart. He believed what God said and God credited that response from Abraham's hearing heart as righteousness.

The moment Abraham heard and believed, in that instant he was transformed and made completely righteous. Because of Abraham's wonderful hearing heart and faith response, he became the model for every one of us. He is now our father in faith.

All faith comes from hearing God, and God is speaking to us continuously. For this reason the writer of Hebrews gives us this solemn warning: *"See to it that you do not refuse Him who speaks"* (Hebrews 12:25). The New American Standard Version translates this verse, *"... Him who is speaking ..."* It doesn't say, "Him who occasionally speaks." If God is speaking, then we need to hear. Most of the time, our ears are too dull. We don't hear. But when we listen attentively to God with an earnest desire to obey Him, with a heart that's genuinely ready to respond to Him no matter what the cost, then faith rises up.

Just as hearing was created to detect sound and sight enables us to detect light, so the purpose of our faith is to see, understand, and respond to the eternal realm – to the One Eternal God. Our five senses put us in contact with the physical world; our faith puts us in contact with the spiritual world.

The living, active Word of God

One way Christians can experience healing is by using the Word of God to do effective warfare against infirmity.

> *"For the Word of God is living and powerful, and sharper than any two-edged sword, piercing even to the division of soul and spirit, and of joints and marrow, and is a discerner of the thoughts and intents of the heart."* (Hebrews 4:12)

That's quite a weapon. When God speaks His powerful word to us, along with that revelation from Him comes tremendous ability and power. This power and ability is able to destroy all that hinders healing.

One of the greatest battles we as Christians must wage is the battle of passivity, the inclination to lay back and allow the enemy to walk all over us. We need to fight the good fight of faith. A "good fight" is one where you are on the "right" side. When a lion attacked one of David's lambs, what did David do? He ripped the lion's jaws apart. When we become ill we need to resist that invasion and assault on our well-being with all our spiritual (and natural) resources.

The Greek word in Hebrews 4:12 translated "living" is *zoë* which means "life of God". In other words, it will never die. Other translations of Hebrews also describe it as "active". Active stems from the Greek word *energos* – working, toiling, effective. So, an amplification of this passage could read:

> *"The Word of God is alive, actively alive. It is filled with the life of God, and is full of His energy. It toils and works in us and is operative and effectual."*

The writer of Hebrews goes on to say that it is also "piercing". That word in Greek means "competent, ample, sufficient, attaining the desired purpose". Adding that to our amplification of these verses, it now reads:

> *"It is sharp enough and is fully competent (adequate, sufficient, ample and has enough ability) to channel itself through the various areas of the soul and spirit, reaching its desired end and attaining its desired goal. It is fully adequate. It will arrive! And it will accomplish its goal once it gets there!"*

Wow! What a promise. The next part speaks of the division of soul and spirit. The word "division" comes from the Greek word *merismes* and means "separation or distribution". It also means to divide, to apportion. We desperately need to experience the Word of God separating out the promises that God has spoken into our life from all the lies of the enemy that have taken root. God's Word can separate them out and cut away what is not needed.

Finally, we read the phrase *"and be able to judge"*, in verse 12. The word "judge" in Greek is *kerithikos* and it means "to judge or critique". Adding these thoughts to our amplification of these verses, we can now render them:

"The Word of God is alive, actively alive. It is filled with the life of God and is full of His energy. It toils and works in us and is operative and effectual. It is sharp enough and fully competent (adequate, sufficient, ample, has enough ability) to channel itself through the various areas of the soul and spirit, reaching its desired end and attaining its desired goal. It will arrive and will accomplish its goal once it gets there! It will divide between soul and spirit, apportioning to each what is needed, as it critiques the thoughts and intentions of the heart. When necessary, it sets the knife to the throat of anything found in the soul that is contrary to His Word."

Amen! Isn't this an exciting way to do effective warfare in releasing people from sickness? Fully contemplate your natural reality, whatever it is – but don't stop there. Superimpose God's blueprint from His Word over the devil's plans and you will surely see the victory.

Victory over needles

In my home city of Victoria, British Columbia, several inter- cessors have been praying that God's blueprint for our city be superimposed over the devil's plans. In the center of the city, the battle has been raging with great intensity. Drugs, prostitution and crime have gained quite a strong foothold. One night, our healing team went right in to the enemy's headquarters.

The place is called, simply, "The Needle Exchange". It is a government-funded project in the inner city of Victoria – a place where hardcore drug addicts can exchange dirty, used needles for new ones and perhaps receive some advice or counseling. It was four days before Christmas when we arrived. Steve Bradley had extended the invitation. Steve, a Christian and an ex- offender had been asked to head up a meeting for addicts, offenders, and people suffering from AIDS, right there in the government-sponsored project. When the invitation came, Steve had simply stated, "You realize, of course, that if I hold meetings they will be explicitly Christian ones." "That's okay," the officials replied, "Word has come to us that your work is a good one and these people need all the help we can get them." So he went and Christ went with him. He has been holding three meetings per week there for almost a year now.

Steve in turn, extended an invitation to us and so there we were, four days before Christmas! The exchange was located in a dark, dreary back alley. Lining the walls were pimps, prostitutes, addicts, people with sunken, haunted eyes, and dealers busy on their cell phones. There were furtive glances, nods of recognition. "Welcome to Christmas in the inner city," someone muttered.

The door opened to a cold, damp cavernous series of rooms. Most people rushed in, exchanged needles at the front counter then quickly disappeared into the night. But some lingered. The ones that remained led us into an inner room more depressing than the first. Paintings of grotesque nudes, garish pictures and AIDS posters all together delivered their explicit, graphic warnings.

The meeting began with a Scripture reading and some simple worship, and suddenly we were caught up. We were enveloped, surrounded by God's presence. Into this most desperate of places, in this threatening, hostile environment, He settled. A place of filth and darkness became holy ground, the atmosphere overflowing with warmth, love and security. Perhaps there were angels there, too? I suppose there were. But what matters is that a blanket of God's love hovered, brooded over us and covered us. That night nothing – no principality, no stronghold of darkness – could bring any harm.

Then the healing started. The first one was a man who had been crippled in an accident. He was a former athlete, now an alcoholic, suffering from advanced arthritis and osteoporosis, with nerve damage and chronic pain. He was healed instantly. He was incredulous and jumped around, pain free, joyous in his new-found liberty. Then there were others, weeping, sobbing, "I'm free! It's gone. The pain is gone." Someone with AIDS exclaimed, "Fire is going through my veins." Then a man with cancer was touched by God. More people with deadly addictions began sobbing, weeping with gratitude. Alcohol problems ... neurological damage ... It seemed that nothing could stand before the awesome might of God that night.

And then it was over. "Another meeting tomorrow night," Steve reminded them.

We realized that God really had come to meet with the poor, the hurting, the desperate, the broken and the lowly. This wasn't about making people happy and sticking some silly grins on their faces. It was about being real. For all the lost, lonely and dying, the reality is that a man called Jesus, 2,000 years ago, died on a real cross and suffered real, intense pain. He shed real blood. He died and rose again, and today He really does heal hurting and broken people – even the most broken of us – especially the most broken of us!

Priorities

One night after a healing/miracle meeting a young lady approached me with the following question, "Why don't I see healings and miracles when I pray for people? I have asked God for this gift. I attempt to walk in integrity and righteousness. I pray for the sick regularly. I exercise faith. Still, I seem to have little or no results."

Before I could answer her, I sensed the Lord speaking to me. "Tell her that unless she makes healing and the miraculous – these necessary manifestations of the Kingdom of God – her first priority, along with My righteousness, there is no guarantee she will ever see people healed." This came as a real revelation to me.

I feel that this instruction/admonition is for many people in the Body of Christ. The reason we are not seeing people healed is because we have other things that we consider to be more important. Healing, along with other spiritual gifts, are often viewed as "optional extras". They're of high, but not utmost importance.

First things first

> *"Seek first the kingdom of God and His righteousness, and all these things shall be added to you."*   (Matthew 6:33)

What is the thing that takes first priority in your life? Where is your first allegiance? Is it your local congregation? That sounds pretty good. Is it maybe, pleasing others? Church growth? How about your family? Your children? Job security? As believers, seeking the Kingdom of God must be our number one priority. While that might not be a revelation to you, the importance of this admonition might be. It is absolutely imperative!

Jesus commanded us to seek the Kingdom *first*. This is not an option, but rather our prime responsibility. Healings, miracles, signs and wonders will follow. They are absolutely necessary Kingdom manifestations and are to be earnestly sought after, but only in the context of an "outflowing" of the Kingdom. If His Kingdom here on earth doesn't occupy our thoughts and imaginations, our time and energy, then just maybe we need to question our priorities.

So, what happens if God's Kingdom is not number one? Two things:

1. The "other things" Jesus promised are no longer guaranteed – not food, not drink, not clothing, nothing!
2. When the Kingdom is number two we become guilty of idolatry. It really is that important.

Here's a handy check list for you, inspired by Norm Brinkley. How do you measure up?

- "Kingdom First Christians" (hereafter referred to as KFCs, but not to be confused with a brand of fried chicken!) are desperate to be used of God in a Kingdom setting together with manifestations of the Kingdom of God such as healing and the prophetic. When we truly put the concerns of the Kingdom first, considerations of self rapidly diminish.
- KFCs desire to advance the Kingdom with the whole world in mind and the whole Gospel in our mouths and in our actions. Among leaders, praying regularly with and for other pastors and other Christian leaders is not unusual – in fact, it's considered one of the highest priorities the Lord gives to us (1 Timothy 2:1–8).

- KFCs realize that it is impossible for their own congregations by themselves to preach, to reach, serve, evangelize, and disciple the "ethnos" (people groups of the world) without the partnership of other congregations and para-church organizations.
- KFCs realize there is a need for a leadership structure that is servant-motivated and miracle-oriented.
- KFCs rejoice when other ministries grow and when signs and wonders follow their preaching.
- KFCs care as much about other ministries as they care about their own.
- KFCs are focused and unified around Jesus and are not motivated by competition or personal agendas.
- KFCs are concerned about the welfare of their whole communities, not just their individual congregations. They believe that churches which reach out and come together in Christ will, as a team, reach far more of lost souls than will the combined efforts of the individual congregations working separately.

We at the Extreme Healing Ministry really believe that too. We want to develop the discipline of proclaiming the Gospel wherever we are and of praying for each other, each others' families and each others' ministries. We seek to develop the priority of preaching the Good News together with signs following. We want to bring the magnificence of Jesus to the home, to the Church and to marketplace. Then the Holy Spirit can do His work in us and through us together.

Note

1. Harris, R. Laird et al., *Theological Wordbook of the Old Testament*, vol. 2, Chicago: Moody Press, 1980, p. 917.

Chapter 4

God's Sovereignty

Although God is sovereign and He does what He wills, still He usually chooses to limit Himself to working through useable mortal vessels. Anointed believing is a key that releases God's sovereign power and ability into our daily lives.

The question

Short of heaven, are we ever going to experience a time and place where everybody gets healed? Are great, eager crowds of people going to pack into a meeting sometime where hundreds of people arrive in wheelchairs, then after the service is over, all those wheelchairs get donated to charity? This side of heaven, will any minister for Christ ever stroll through the wards of a sprawling hospital complex in a big American city and see every single patient rise out of bed whole and in glowing health? Or will we ever get to the point where we see miracles more numerous and more marvelous than any of those during Jesus' ministry?

Yet Jesus said,

> "I tell you the truth, anyone who has faith in me will do what I have been doing. He will do even greater things than these, because I am going to the Father."   (John 14:12 NIV)

Some and not others

The question, on occasion, arises, "Since God is sovereign, and since we don't at present see everyone healed, are we therefore correct in assuming that God does not want to heal certain individuals?" In other words, is there something about God's overriding will that determines who gets healed and when? Is the exercise of faith always the determining factor?

Allow me to answer, firstly, by exposing some misconceptions about God's sovereignty. What does it really mean when we say that God is sovereign? His word clearly says that He hears and answers our prayers. So when we say that God is sovereign, and yet sometimes He decides it is not His will to heal a person at a certain time, are we not saying, in so many words, that God's sovereignty overrides His word? That is to say, that His word is one factor, but the particular individual, the specific time and the place, even the people praying, are all variables. Sound good? Not quite! His word is *always* His word. God obligates Himself to keep His word – every jot and every tittle thereof – or He isn't God! I cannot have faith in a God who won't do what He says He'll do, can I?

I am convinced that God's sovereignty is one of the most abused and misunderstood truths in all of Christianity! Further, I am convinced that God's sovereignty has been blamed for more of the devil's work than any single act the Liar himself has committed. People frequently, in fact, blame human failure on God's sovereignty.

There's a true story of an American Air Force pilot instructor attempting to train two Muslim would-be pilots. One or the other of the students would do something wrong and the flight instructor would try to correct him. The reply was always the same, "Allah wills." Another mistake, another attempt at correction, and again the same reply, "Allah wills." Every correction was met with, "Allah wills"! The conclusion? They, themselves, made no mistakes. Everything was the "will of God"! The Church, too, frequently thinks like that.

Sometimes, there's no healing because of "corporate" weakness. The New Testament is filled with examples of local churches whose middle-pew members struggled with basic issues such as false doctrines, sexual immorality, and disorder. In Corinthians Paul admonishes the local church on such issues and identifies that it is a barrier to healing:

"In the first place, I hear that when you come together as a church, there are divisions among you, and to some extent I believe it. No doubt there have to be differences among you to show which of you have God's approval. When you come together, it is not the Lord's Supper you eat, for as you eat, each of you goes ahead without waiting for anybody else. One remains hungry, another gets drunk. Don't you have homes to eat and drink in? Or do you despise the church of God and humiliate those who have nothing? What shall I say to You? Shall I praise you for this? Certainly not!"   (1 Corinthians 11:18–22 NIV)

There are plenty of other examples in God's Word where the local churches fall short of God's plan for them. Are we really behaving so much better today?

God looks down at His Church, His Son's body on earth, and His heart is to heal every person. But He sees the state the body is in, the selfishness, the sin, the idolatry. His body is just not at a place where it is able to receive healing fully and completely.

Whatever the issues and reasons might be, we sometimes walk out of healing services, not carrying our beds, but carrying the same infirmities we brought in. In fact, we do it on a pretty frequent basis. And our response often is: "I prayed. Others prayed for me. But I didn't get healed. So, since God is sovereign, it must not have been His will to heal me."

Yet we are a people God is absolutely passionate about. He has big plans for us. And His blessings are always there, always here. It says in 2 Corinthians 12:9 that His grace is sufficient for us. But just in case that isn't enough for you, His grace isn't just sufficient, in fact it *abounds* (2 Corinthians 9:8)!

Tension is the thing

As with many biblical truths, it seems, there is a tension at work here. On the one hand, the Scriptures teach that God is the unlimited, sovereign, reigning Lord who has reconciled the world to Himself through His Son, the Messiah. On the other, we understand that we do not yet see all things under Jesus' feet.

One day every knee will bow (Philippians 2:10–11), but until that day, God's people operate under Christ's delegated authority. We've heard the preacher who holds up a Bible and announces, "I've read the last page, and we win!" Yes, indeed. But much more: that ultimate victory is God working out His plans for every single person's life perfectly. There really will be no loose ends left behind when we are swept up into glory.

In the workings of this Divine master plan, we sometimes assume, or perhaps we would just like to believe, that God overrides or bypasses human initiative and that the devil is completely under control in this season. This is not what the Scriptures say. If this were true, then why have the Church as the representative of God's authority?

Why did Jesus come down and heal the sick? Had the Father sovereignly allowed those people to be ill? Why did the Son cast out demons? Did His Father send the devils into those people in the first place, or at least allow them access to those poor souls?

Some people's view of God's sovereignty is fatalistic. If God is sovereign and we are sick, why seek healing? If we are deaf, why have people lay on hands and pray for us? Why wear hearing aids or undergo emergency appendectomies? Or jump out of the way of that speeding Toyota? If God is controlling everything, then we certainly would do best to leave everything the way it is – wouldn't we?

Paul's pesky problem

People sometimes ask me about Paul's thorn in the flesh. And about Timothy whom Paul admonished to take a little wine for frequent stomach ailments? They arch their eyebrows. Aren't these exceptions? Is sickness not an indication of sin? If we are supposed to prosper, then why did Jesus not have a place to lay His head? Didn't He earn His keep? Why did most or all of His disciples die for their faith? And so on, and so forth.

My response to such questions is one I find myself using a lot when helping my sons with their homework: I don't know! And in this case, it's quite true. We can probably thank God, I suppose, that I claim no special or divine revelation in this or any other area! But as far as Paul is concerned, I do believe that Scripture is very clear, that his thorn in the flesh was not a sickness, but a messenger of Satan, sent to stir up opposition and persecution wherever he ministered. In fact, as we follow the life of Saul-turned-Paul, we hear of beatings, shipwrecks, trials and imprisonment. The man paid an incredible price to give his testimony before emperors and kings. But there is no evidence, along the way, of prolonged bouts of debilitating sickness. Paul was simply too busy to be sick, too busy going about the Father's business.

In addition, it is significant that Paul urged Timothy to seek a natural remedy for his sickness, not just to accept it as God's will. Doesn't it follow, then, that if Timothy didn't recover, Paul would subsequently have prayed for his friend for a supernatural healing? We have no record of Paul ever saying, "Your sickness is God's will so don't even think about trying to recover."

Rebel territory

There is a teaching around that says that God sovereignly "allows" people to be sick, and further that the devil cannot make a move or do anything, unless God the Father sovereignly and specifically wills it. Where would such an attitude leave us? It would leave us without the ministry of the Son.

Jesus came to earth, and as He moved among us, He absolutely devastated sickness and evil. He said, in effect, "I come representing, completely and perfectly, the will of God. I represent His rule, His total Lordship. When you look at me you see God's rule in operation. You see My Father's heart. Are you sick? Be healed! Are you demonized? Be delivered! Are you hungry? Be fed! Are you naked? Be clothed! Are you poor? Receive of My abundance! And now, go in My name and do the same!" This is Christ's mandate to us: to represent Him accurately. To show people what His Father – our Father – is like. Why? So that people can truly know the Father and His character.

Hebrews 1:2 (NIV) says, *"In these last days he has spoken to us by his Son, whom he appointed heir of all things."* God's will is fully disclosed in Jesus, in both His actions and in His words. They disclose that His Father is the Supreme Ruler, but that there are pockets of "rebel territory" on planet earth where God's will is not fully carried out. Further, we are shown that sickness and disease interrupt and impair the outworking of the will of God.

When Jesus came into Peter's house one day, the Bible tells us, *"he saw Peter's mother-in-law lying in bed with a fever. He touched her hand and the fever left her, and she got up and began to wait on him"* (Matthew 8:14–15 NIV).

Note, please, that Jesus didn't stroll in, spot the bedridden lady then loudly exclaim to all and sundry how wonderful it was that His Father in heaven was developing this lady's character through her illness (although He does develop character through suffering). He didn't then applaud her long-suffering, forgive her sins (even though He had been known to do so on other occasions), and then go about His business. He quickly and simply saw her need, reached out and healed her. And then she, for her part, rose up and got to work. She went about her Father's business.

We are susceptible to a fatalistic type of sovereignty thinking which might be more pagan than scriptural as it robs the Church of both its mandate and its authority. Instead of crying out, "Where are the miracles of our forefathers?" people say, "Don't you know that God is sovereign? Don't you know that He's got the devil on a leash?"

Try telling that to David Hogan and to the 200 former corpses who are now vital and alive through his ministry! Or is it only the corpses of the Western world who are to remain in the ground, what with God's sovereignty and Western culture being what they are?

We have been robbed! We are not to look back with envy on the New Testament Church and all its miracles. We *are* a New Testament Church!

Do you remember 1 Peter 5:8? The devil is depicted as a roaring, devouring lion. It is always healthy to deal with that fellow – with all evil – on a practical, detailed, specific-incident-by-specific-incident basis. For instance, what man of us relaxing in a city park with his young daughter playing nearby, if he sees her suddenly attacked, would drop his Bible crossword puzzle book, fall to his knees, and prayerfully consider God's will in the matter of her life and limb? Utter nonsense. Every one of us would race instantly to her rescue without thinking.

What would any of us do, further, if we saw a brother or a sister or a wife or a child beginning to fall into demonic deception through a cult? Would we consider very carefully that perhaps that particular loved one was destined by the will of God to eternal damnation? Again, lunacy. We would start that very hour to wage spiritual warfare!

In Ezekiel 22:30 (NIV), we read, *"I looked for a man among them who would build up the wall and stand before me in the gap on behalf of the land so I would not have to destroy it, but I found none."* If that verse means anything, it means that one man, one woman, one young person can change the destiny of things. Just one! God is compelled to act in perfect justice if no one calls on Him for mercy. Intercession is calling on God to be merciful.

So, is God sovereign? Sure. But in His sovereignty He usually chooses to work through His children. We are His hands and feet. We are His approved workmen. If we want to see His Kingdom flourish, we must be proactive.

A scripture picture

From Genesis to Revelation, Scripture is full of examples where both man's initiative and God's sovereignty are found in the same passage. Here we see God's sovereignty held in proper tension:

Man's initiative	God's sovereignty
Draw near to God and	He will draw near to you (James 4:8)
Work out your salvation	for it is God who works in you (Philippians 2:12–13)
Seek the LORD	while He may be found (Isaiah 55:6)
Call upon Him	while He is near (Psalm 145:18)

Man's initiative	God's sovereignty
I sought the LORD	and He heard me and healed me (Psalm 34:4)
Abraham prayed to God	and God healed Abimelech (Genesis 20:17)
(She) sought deliverance for her daughter	Jesus delivered her (Mark 7:24–30)
Crowds followed	Jesus healed them all (Matthew 12:15)

There is another way to compare our role with that of God.

Vital side	Legal side
Has to do with our experience	Has to do with the cross, with the law, with what God did
Has to do with man's initiative	Has to do with God's sovereignty
Living, experiential relationship	Covenant; a legal agreement

Don't be cruel

I've seen some people in ministry acting very uncharitably towards people who have not been healed. They've said things such as: "It's your fault; it's unbelief; if only you had more faith (we've all been told that, I think); you're not doing enough; you have sin in your life (which is true for the vast majority of humankind anyway); you have demonic bondage" etc. They blame the sick person themselves. How unkind! Look at all the incidents where Jesus got angry and upbraided people. In every incident stubborn pride and deep opposition were involved. Usually it was the ones who should have known better – the leaders, the ones who claimed to "know".

But the abuse of some peoples' ministry of healing doesn't mean that we, ourselves, shouldn't continue to use the gifts (including healing and deliverance) properly. Abuse shouldn't result in non-use.

Why heal, anyway?

We are healed simply because God wants to heal us. That much is clear. But there is so, so much more to it. Ultimately, every good and perfect deed, act, or gift goes to the glory of God. Yes, that's key. But there are still other important reasons why God's healing power is active on this earth.

The gospel of John, chapter 9, tells of a particularly note-worthy day – if that can really be said – in the life of Jesus on this earth. On their way from one place to another, His disciples pointed out to Him a blind man. They asked Jesus why he was blind, and whose sin had caused it? Jesus replied that the blindness wasn't on account of any sin. He then healed the man. The Jewish establishment was not amused, especially since it was the Sabbath. They hauled the once-sightless man up for questioning. His answers only made them angrier. The remarkable story continues:

> *"The Jews still did not believe that he had been blind and had received his sight until they sent for the man's parents. 'Is this your son?' they asked. 'Is this the one you say was born blind? How is it that now he can see?'*
>
> *'We know he is our son,' the parents answered, 'and we know that he was born blind. But how he can see now, or who opened his eyes, we don't know. Ask him. He is of age, he will speak for himself.' His parents said this because they were afraid of the Jews, for already the Jews had decided that anyone who acknowledged that Jesus was the Christ would be put out of the synagogue. That was why his parents said, 'He is of age, ask him.'*
>
> *A second time they summoned the man who had been blind. 'Give glory to God,' they said. 'We know that this man [Jesus] is a sinner.'*
>
> *He replied, 'Whether he is a sinner or not, I don't know. One thing I do know. I was blind but now I see!'*

Then they asked him, 'What did he do to you? How did he open your eyes?'

He answered, 'I have told you already and you did not listen. Why do you want to hear it again? Do you want to become his disciples, too?'

Then they hurled insults at him and said, 'You are this fellow's disciple! We are disciples of Moses! We know that God spoke to Moses, but as for this fellow, we don't even know where he comes from.'

The man answered, 'Now that is remarkable! You don't know where he comes from, yet he opened my eyes. We know that God does not listen to sinners. He listens to the godly man who does his will. Nobody has ever heard of opening the eyes of a man born blind. If this man were not from God, he could do nothing.'

To this they replied, 'You were steeped in sin at birth; how dare you lecture us!' And they threw him out.

Jesus heard that they had thrown him out, and when he found him, he said, 'Do you believe in the Son of Man?'

'Who is he, sir?' the man asked. 'Tell me so that I may believe in him.'

Jesus said, 'You have now seen him; in fact, he is the one speaking with you.'

Then the man said, 'Lord, I believe,' and he worshipped him."

(John 9:18–38 NIV)

We see here three more reasons for healing on this earth. Firstly, the blind man's healing experience made him bold. Secondly, it gave him an experiential testimony that confounded the wisdom of the wise. And lastly, it led to his salvation!

'Cause the Bible tells us so

I believe that the main reason we aren't healed is not tied up in the incomprehensible nature of the sovereignty of God. Instead, what God has done for us legally and judicially has not been fully apprehended by us in an experiential and vital way. But we mustn't be discouraged. This is the incentive we all share: to seek continuously, to learn, to grow, and to expect from God. If you listen to nothing else I say, please hear that.

Paul said, *"He was delivered over to death for our sins, and raised to life for our justification* (Romans 4:25 NIV) and, *"Therefore, since we have been justified through faith, we have peace with God through our Lord Jesus Christ"* (Romans 5:1 NIV).

That experience, that deed in history, is ours to receive. The death on the cross of the Lamb of God, is become a vital, present experience. It brings us into possession of new things. Among those new things is peace with God *and* healing (1 Peter 2:24).

God meets us where we are. If we, many times through no fault of our own, are unable to receive as did the blind-since-birth man in John, He still pours out as much grace and tenderness as we are able to receive. Often times people have great ability to receive in ways other than physical healing – in such areas, for example, as love, in intimacy, consolation, in giving, in encouragement, in strength for family and loved ones, even in anointing to minister to others in the midst of suffering, sickness and death.

We aren't all healed. But there will come that day, if it hasn't already arrived, when, as it says in John 14:12, we will see greater works, greater healings, than those of Jesus' time. We will. God's Word has told us so. And, in the meantime, our heavenly Father meets us wherever we are. His grace is sufficient for us in every situation. His favor is upon us. And His love for us through His Holy Spirit is for every day we spend on this earth and for all eternity afterward.

Chapter 5

Tried, Tested and Blue

... Black and blue, that is. Christians have endured being battered and bruised from time to time. Even frequently. Why? Is it some sort of test? The apostle Peter in his first epistle, teaches on faith that undergoes testing. He tells us that the trial of our faith, which is more precious than gold that perishes, though it is tested with fire, will be a praise, honor and glory at the appearing of Jesus Christ (1 Peter 1:7).

Faith that is not tested is not particularly useful. I recently heard one Bible teacher share how he felt led to plant a church in another city because he wanted to be somewhere where he had to exercise faith. He had become so complacent and so self-sufficient that he rarely had to exercise faith. I want to be in a place where it is necessary to exercise faith every day and not just once a day, but many times a day. Faith that is tested and has stood the test becomes operational faith.

Verse 5 of this same chapter in 1 Peter says we are, "... *kept by the power of God through faith for salvation ready to be revealed in the last time.*" There is a great salvation which is to be revealed in the end times. We are now in those very times. Last days events are rapidly unfolding. Salvation is much more than having our sins forgiven and making it into the rapture. This "great salvation" encompasses the forgiveness of sins, holiness, the baptism of the Holy Spirit, a tasting of the power of the age to come, i.e. healing, miracles, and even resurrection from the dead. All of this is made operational through faith that has been tested and found to be true.

God tests us not to harm us, not to cause us grief, not to do us evil, but rather so that we may grow, that we might pass the test

45

and go on to bear more fruit in our lives. What does it mean to test something? It means to put pressure on it to see if it will do what it is intended to do. Will it hold up under stress? Can it perform according to the manufacturer's specifications? Is it authentic when measured against a true standard of quality or excellence?

God does this with us. When we go through such difficulties and pressures things happen inside. We experience inner change. Motives are revealed – and purified. The desire to sin is burnt away. The apostle Peter said, *"He who has suffered in the flesh has ceased from sin"* (1 Peter 4:1). Sin doesn't have the appeal it once had. We are different. We have different motives.

What's the real price?

We need to count the cost. We need to realize more fully just what it is we are asking for when we ask for God's strength and power to flow through us. David said this about the Lord, *"He weakened my strength in the way* [in the process]*"* (Psalm 102:23). What about Jacob? God weakened his natural strength, too. Remember the limp? We cry to God for strength and wham! Something unexpected and not too pleasant hits us. Great pressure comes upon us. We are bent down. And then God speaks, *"My power is reserved for those who have no strength!"*

God evaluates us. He chooses and calls us. In the Scriptures, the word *choose* means to be selected for more blessing as a result of "passing the test" or "making the grade".

The prophet Isaiah quotes God as saying to us, *"I have tried and chosen you in the furnace of affliction"* (Isaiah 48:10 AMP). Again that word "chosen" means graded, promoted. It's like a child going from the first grade into the second grade. God says, "I've caused you to graduate, to go on to the next level or grade." Jesus said, *"Many are called, but few are chosen"* (Matthew 22:14). Not being chosen doesn't mean losing your salvation, by the way. It relates to usefulness or fruit. Are you bearing fruit? Can you be entrusted with more, with greater responsibility in the Kingdom?

Who's up to the task? Why are so few chosen? Because most fail the test in the furnace and they have to repeat the grade. If you are at a place right now in your life where nothing seems to make much sense, trust God anyway! The Psalmist says, *"Trust, lean on, rely on and have confidence in Him at all times, you people; pour out your heart before Him. God is a refuge for us – a fortress and a high tower"* (Psalm 62:8, AMP). Notice that the trust God expects us to have in Him is not occasional or sporadic, but at all times.

Chill out

Paul encouraged his son in the faith, Timothy:

> *"I am calling up memories of your sincere and unqualified faith (the leaning of your entire personality on God in Christ in absolute trust and confidence of His power, wisdom and good-ness), [a faith] that first lived permanently [in the heart of] your grandmother Lois and your mother Eunice and now, I am [fully] persuaded, [dwells] in you also."*

> (2 Timothy 1:5 AMP)

Paul was saying, 'Timothy, your faith may be tested, but trust con-tinuously, leaning your entire personality on God's faithfulness."

This is the way the power of the gospel works. So, when pressure comes, relax! Out of your inability, God can work His ability. The principle is this: God's strength comes through when you are in trouble. God says, *"My strength is made perfect in weakness"* (2 Corinthians 12:9).

We can understand now why Paul said, *"Therefore, I will boast all the more gladly about my weaknesses so that Christ's power may rest on me"* (verse 9 continued). In other words, "That is why, for Christ's sake, I delight in weaknesses." Was Paul a masochist? Absolutely not! *"In insults,"* he goes on, *"in hardships, in persecu-tions, in difficulties. For when I am weak, then I am strong"* (verse 10 NIV).

We must recognize that contrary and difficult circumstances in our lives are not necessarily the devil. Often, they are the merciful hand of the Lord seeking to do deeper, more marvelous things in our lives. In the furnace of affliction some will pass the test. Some will make the grade and receive the promotion. May we be included in that. One day the Lord will say, *"You have been faithful over a few things. I will make you ruler over many things"* (Matthew 25:23).

Again 1 Peter 1:5 tells us that we are kept by this power, this energy of God, through faith (through continuous, anointed believing) unto salvation. This means that the moment you are saved and filled with the Holy Spirit, God put more than enough spiritual energy and dynamic power in you to blast you through all the power of Satan. Nothing can stop you as you carry out the will of God. *"I can do all things through Christ who strengthens me"* (Philippians 4:13).

God expects this power to be displayed in the Church. Jesus worked the works of His Father performing many miracles of healing. This is how He expressed it to His disciples, in effect: "You see all these things I have done? I want you to replicate these very things" (John 14:12). How do we do it? Through the Holy Spirit.

So what is the price? What is the cost of having the power and authority of the Son of God to speak into lives? It is weakness. It is testing. It is trial. It is persecution. It is tribulation. It is sometimes even martyrdom. And the reward? Effective ministry and all that that means: healings and salvations, an increase to the Kingdom, and a glory which shall be revealed in us which far, far exceed those costs we will ever pay on this earth (Romans 8:18).

Bombs away

Recently a friend of mine and his son went skydiving. For them it was an extremely exhilarating experience! I've had the same euphoria, and I haven't had to climb to 5,000 feet to experience it. Over the past several years especially, I've had to jump out, so to speak, many times; take "leaps" of faith. And each and every time, God swooped down and rescued me before I hit bottom. Wow! If you want to be a Kingdom extender, you have got to do it too. Trust Him, then launch out. With God nothing is impossible (Luke 1:37).

Smith Wigglesworth is sometimes called the *apostle of faith*. He believed the Scriptures, that nothing was impossible with God. He really believed it. His remarkable faith was an inspiration to many. One special surge of faith occurred while he was staying in a small place, in the home of the curate of the local Church of England church.

Wigglesworth and the curate were sitting together talking after supper. No doubt the subject of their conversation was that the poor fellow had no legs. Artificial limbs in those days were unlike the sophisticated limbs of today.

Wigglesworth said to the man quite suddenly, which he often did when ministering in cases like this, "Go and get a new pair of shoes in the morning."

The poor fellow thought it was some kind of joke. However, after Wigglesworth and the curate had retired to their respective rooms for the night, God said to the curate, "Do as my servant hath said." What a designation for any person – *My servant!* God was identifying Himself with Wigglesworth.

There was no more sleep for the man that night. He rose up early, went downtown, and stood waiting for the shoe shop to open. The manager eventually arrived and opened the shop for business. The curate went in and sat down. Presently, an assistant came and said, "Good morning, sir. Can I help you?"

The man said, "Yes, would you get me a pair of shoes, please."

"Yes, sir. Size and colour?"

The curate hesitated. The assistant then saw his condition and said, "I'm sorry, sir. We can't help you."

"It's alright, young man. But I do want a pair of shoes. Size 8, colour black."

The assistant went to get the requested shoes. A few minutes later he returned and handed them to the man. The man put one stump into a shoe, and instantly a foot and leg formed! Then the same thing happened with the other leg!

He walked out of that shop, not only with a new pair of shoes, but also with a new pair of legs!

Wigglesworth was not surprised. He had expected the result. He often made remarks like this, "As far as God is concerned, there is no difference between forming a limb and healing a broken bone."[1]

Another marvellous man of faith was Dr. Charles Price. Originally from England and trained in law at Wesley College, Oxford, Dr. Price challenged people to recognize the difference between emotion and the anointing of the Holy Spirit. Dr. Price had a conversion experience at a Free Methodist mission in Spokane, Washington. Later, he attended Aimee Semple McPherson's meetings in San Jose, California, and was filled with the Holy Spirit. From that moment on he became a blazing flame of faith and a releaser of divine healing wherever he went. Price was a powerful evangelist who often had one thousand conversions per day in his campaigns. His pattern was to go into a community and stay until "the heavens opened". Here is what he says about faith:

Real faith that weighs no more than a mustard seed will do more than a ton of will and determination. For you can no more have real faith without result than the sun can shine without light. Now since real faith never fails to bring about the result, what is it that we have mistakenly called faith? Simply put, *we have failed to understand the difference between faith and belief...*

... Therein lies our difficulty. We have made faith a condition of the mind, when it is a divinely imparted grace of the heart. Beloved, we have been wrong in our attitude and practice. When the sunlight of God's grace and truth floods our hearts and minds, there will be an end to our struggling, and these hearts of ours will be wrapped in His garment of peace. In that hour, we'll realize that *we can receive faith only as He gives it.* No longer will we struggle to believe. In the Galilee storm, the disciples could have worked themselves into a frenzy trying to still its fury. But just three words from Jesus, "Peace. Be still" (Mark 4:39), and the wind dropped from a scream to a whisper, and the wind and sea obeyed Him ...

... When I want faith, I must seek Him. I can't get it anywhere but from that matchless One of whom it is said, *"He is the author and finisher of our faith."*

The thing above all else I want you to see is that you cannot generate faith, you cannot work it up, and you cannot manufacture it. God Himself must impart it. You cannot obtain faith by struggling or by affirming that something is, nor can you turn your hope and desire into faith by your own power. You can only get faith from the Lord, for the Word clearly states that faith is one of two things – a gift of God or a fruit of the Spirit.[2]

Notes

1. Madden, Peter J., *The Wigglesworth Standard*, Whitaker House, 1993. pp. 19–20.
2. Price, Charles, *The Real Faith for Healing*, Logos Publishing, Plainfield, N.J.

Chapter 6

Hard at Rest

I have written in an earlier chapter that much more than self-worth, we Christians need *identity*. Oh, how we need identity! Oh, how we need to be freed from an orphan spirit and a lack of knowing who we are and 'whose' we are. In the natural, when we don't really know who we are and whose we are, we are *driven*. This driven-ness leads us to *do* things to try and establish our identity or to try to find our identity in *doing* things. We strive to conquer, to accomplish, or to perform in order to feel valuable.

In the book of Acts, Jesus told Paul, *"It is hard to kick against the goads"* (Acts 9:5). Christians are for the most part, I feel, not at rest in their souls. And it's not all the exertion or hard work that's doing it. The soul doesn't fatigue. The soul has an indestructible life. The rest for our soul comes when we stop struggling against our spirit. The restlessness in our soul comes from the need for validation, recognition and love. This need is never satisfied until we find our true identity in Him. "Restless are our hearts until they rest in thee," Augustine said. God said to Moses, *"My presence will go with you"* (Exodus 33:14). Why did God say that? To bring Moses into a place of rest. The writer to the Hebrews instructs us to, *"strive to enter that rest"* (Hebrews 4:11 RSV).

The Bible has many of these seeming paradoxes, like this tension between striving and rest. The deeper truth and meaning is only revealed as we struggle between the two, seemingly contradictory directives: "strive" and "rest". We see occasions of great heroic effort and striving and at other times there's rest, trust and confidence. Power, effort and striving flow out of and lead to rest and intimacy. And, conversely, rest and intimacy bring power, effort and the ability to strive successfully. There is, as Heidi Baker says, "No fruitfulness without intimacy."

God's abundant provision

"Blessed are those who hunger and thirst for righteousness, for they shall be filled." (Matthew 5:6)

The Bible has some important things to say about hunger, especially for those who want to walk in faith. Luke 1:53 (NIV) tells us, *"He has filled the hungry with good things but has sent the rich away empty."* In 1 Corinthians 14:1 (NIV) we read, *"Follow the way of love and eagerly desire* [hunger for] *spiritual gifts."*

To understand the Kingdom of God, we must recognize a couple of facts. Firstly, it's like the huge banquet I described earlier, with an abundance of every nourishing, delicious kind of food. The master of the banquet says, "All may freely eat." There is revealed an important point about the Kingdom of God – that there is absolute abundance. In Ephesians 3:20 we hear of a God who is able to do (or give) *"exceedingly abundantly above all that we ask or think."* That's a lot of adverbs! No one in the Kingdom of God can truly say, "We don't have enough love. We don't have enough joy. We don't have enough healing. We don't have enough faith. We don't have enough food."

The level of God's provision is abundance in everything. One of the most powerful verses in the New Testament tells us that very thing:

"And God is able to make all grace abound to you, so that in all things at all times, having all that you need, you will abound in every good work." (2 Corinthians 9:8 NIV)

Again, notice it is by grace – not by law. So, God has equipped us with all we need and He doesn't expect us to have to fight or grapple to receive it, but to rest in Him and believe His promises to us.

In this verse there are two key words: "abound" and "all". "Abound" occurs twice and "all" – or "every" – occurs five times in that one verse. In no way could the language be more emphatic. When speaking about the level of God's provision for His people, it says, *"All grace . . . so that in all things at all times, having all that you need, you will abound in every good work."* (The last word in English is "every", but in the Greek it is the same word as for "all"). If you have all that you need in all things at all times to abound to every good work, there is absolutely no room for unsupplied need anywhere in your life. This includes all forms of supernatural ministry.

God's provision is on that level. God does not merely offer us just enough. If we, by faith, appropriate His grace, then the level of His provision is abundance. We have more than enough for all our needs and for ourselves.

Take notice that the final purpose of abundance is *"every good work"* (2 Corinthians 9:8). It is not selfish indulgence; it is being able to do good works. What kind? Every kind. This includes supernatural good works. Why does God want His children to have abundance? His specific, practical reason is contained in Acts, where Paul was quoting Jesus: *"The Lord Jesus himself said: 'It is more blessed to give than to receive' "* (Acts 20:35, NIV).

If you want this kind of abundance, which comes by grace, not by law, then you must act in faith, and that means you must give first. The words of Jesus in Luke 6:38 express this idea:

> *"Give, and it will be given to you. A good measure, pressed down, shaken together and running over, will be poured into your lap. For with the measure you use, it will be measured to you."*
>
> (NIV)

Do you want a "good measure" to be given to you? Then you must give first. That is faith. If you are not willing to act in faith, you will not set in motion the processes that will bring God's prosperity, God's power and God's abundance to your ministry.

No favorites?

God has no favorites. Have you heard that expression in the Church? Yes, it's true that God is no respecter of persons and that is confirmed in several scriptural passages, but what does it mean that God is no respecter of persons? It simply means that all have access. All have an equal opportunity to seek and pursue God. But it is those who avail themselves of that opportunity that enjoy God's favor. God will ignore the plans of one person and respond quickly to the cry of another. On what basis does He do so? To the extent that we are in relationship with God and are interacting with Him.

Imagine God loving one twin but hating the other. This was the case with Esau and Jacob. The Bible says, *"Esau I hated – Jacob I loved."* Very strong language! Why did God reject Esau? It was because he despised his birthright, that is, eternal, enduring values. Afterward, even though he sought it with tears, it was too late. Jacob God loved. Why? Because he put a very high value on his birthright, on the supernatural and the eternal. Esau valued only the temporary; only his natural appetites. Jacob enjoyed God's favor. Jacob exercised faith in the goodness of God toward him.

Obtaining favor

The only way to walk in God's favor is to please Him. But what brings pleasure to His heart? Scripture is clear: it is faith (Hebrews 11:6). And this faith that pleases Him is an actual product of knowing Him. Faith is engrafted into our spirits through encountering Him. He is a God of relationship.

The truth is, God takes pleasure in us. He especially takes pleasure in those of us who enjoy Him and pursue Him. "If we draw back," the Word says, "His soul will take no pleasure in us." Draw back from what? From walking with Him – by faith. We posture ourselves to please Him by hungering and thirsting for His presence and His word. This hungering and thirsting requires that we embrace the Word of God as that which reveals Him.

That is why Romans 10:17 tells us, *"Faith comes by hearing, and hearing by the word of God."* The Word of God is not merely sentences written with ink on paper. The Word of God is spiritual power, energy and truth released from the mouth of God. It carries the ability to convey who God is and is, in a sense, God Himself. So, Jesus is called "the Word" of God: *"... and the Word was with God and the Word was God"* (John 1:1).

This brings us ever increasing faith, a commodity that is much more that just strong belief.

God likes us

God appreciates those who pursue Him and who are like Him. The more we resemble Him, the deeper the relationship. When we are newly born again, His mercy pursues us. His intention though is that we become like Him. Although it is true that we will always require mercy, still, friendship with God is the quality to pursue par excellence. The person who has power with God is the person who has a friendship with God. This is the person who enjoys God's favor. To live in the dimension of God's mercy alone is to miss the purpose for life. The intent for which He gave us salvation was for fellowship. Every great man or woman of faith dwelt in a place of friendship with God.

Moses

> *"So the LORD spoke to Moses face to face, as a man speaks to his friend."*   (Exodus 33:11)

Even among the great men and women of God in the Bible, Moses stood out. He had a special place in the Father's heart. He spoke with God as one man speaks with another. God regarded Him as a friend. It was the faith of Moses that brought him to this depth of friendship. Faith is both a pathway to and a product of intimacy with God.

Jesus encouraged the disciples with many insights into His Father's nature. He said,

> *"Do not fear, little flock, for it is your Father's good pleasure to give you the kingdom."*   (Luke 12:32)

He said,

> *"Therefore I say to you, do not worry about your life, what you will eat or what you will drink; nor about your body, what you will put on. Is not life more than food and the body more than clothing? Look at the birds of the air, for they neither sow nor reap nor gather into barns; yet your heavenly Father feeds them. Are you not of more value than they?"*

(Matthew 6:25–26)

This is who God is! When we approach Him knowing these things the shrill whine of unbelief is gone. This is pleasing to Him.

When we choose to believe less of the Lord than He is, that is often what we get. But when our understanding of Him matches who He is, it releases the favor of God. The Lord is honored when out of a clear revelation of His kindness we appeal to His nature. This is faith! Why wait for God to pity us when we can rise in accordance with His plan and call on His name? There is a place of favor reserved for many but enjoyed by few. The time has come for us to choose where we will stand.

Classes of blessing

Thus, we have total favor from our Father. It is this very favor that brings us three classes of blessing that God's Word says are ours. These are very interesting, very practical, and very applicable to our lives as we walk in faith.[1]

1. *Present blessings*. These come to us as soon as we are born again. They are forgiveness of sins, justification, and friendship with God.
2. *Future blessings*. These are the ones that will be ours in eternity. They are ours by inheritance, but we can't enjoy them now. They're in our heavenly bank account. These blessings are our resurrection body, being taken into God's presence forever (the beatific vision, the communion of the saints and complete joy and worship).

3. ***Maybe blessings***. These are blessings that only go to the hungry. Sounds strange, but these are wonderfully, amazingly enormous blessings and they are yours and mine *if* we want them badly enough. These are treasures that are ours by the blood atonement, but they won't come to us unless we are hungry for them, really hungry, and if we make a determined effort to possess them. Some of these *maybe* blessings are:

- Deliverance from all sin patterns, all sin habits and all sins of the flesh; for example, addictions, habits, immorality. There is provision for that in the Kingdom but, sadly, not all receive these blessings.
- Victory over self (or being self-centered). Paul told the church at Rome, *"what I want to do I do not do, but what I hate I do . . . What a wretched man I am! Who will rescue me from this body of death? Thanks be to God – through Jesus Christ our Lord!"* He shows us that freedom from self-preoccupation comes when we focus on the Spirit, not the flesh. (Romans 7:15, 24–25 NIV)
- The constant flow of the Holy Spirit through our personalities. Most of us currently experience interrupted flow.
- The empowering of the Holy Spirit. Acts 1:8 says, *"You shall receive power when the Holy Spirit has come upon you."*
- Productivity (fruitfulness) in Christian service. John 15:16 states, *"You did not choose Me, but I chose you."* Why? To bear fruit.
- Growth in grace and an unimpeded, constant spirit of worship. Romans 12:1 indicates this is unhindered and available to all.

All of the above are like the Promised Land was to Israel. They arrived there. They saw it. They could almost taste it. But Israel had to be hungry enough and desperate enough to want to fight for it. In the end, God would do the fighting, but they had to be willing.

Count me in

Okay, but just how do you receive this *maybe* class of blessings? How does this apply to your life today? Here are some facts about spiritual hunger:

- *You get nothing unless you strive for it.* God doesn't usually force-feed you. What did Joshua do? He fought his way into the Promised Land. He was hungry. What created his hunger? What whetted his appetite? Remember those spies who had gone in before? Today we have spiritual spies – the prophets and intercessors. But remember, as it went with Joshua and Caleb, they won't just turn up milk and honey. Enemies will be lurking about who will challenge our right of possession – enemies of fear, of discouragement, or confusion and distraction.

- *You can have as much as you insist on having.* Some don't know that. God told Joshua, *"Every place on which the sole of your foot treads shall be yours"* (Deuteronomy 11:24). That scripture has filtered down to today's vernacular when you tell someone you are "putting your foot down". It lets them know that you really insist. The spy Caleb conquered the Promised Land, then went to Joshua and insisted on receiving the mountain Moses promised him. And he got it! The daughters of Zelophehad were overlooked in the distribution of the land. They came to Moses and insisted, *"Give us a possession among our father's brothers"* (Numbers 27:4). Moses granted their request. In the gospel of Matthew we read, *"The kingdom of heaven suffers violence, and the violent take it by force"* (Matthew 11:12). Pretty strong words. Fighting words. But they make a hugely important point. Passivity does not honor our Father! Here's the principle: the more daring the request, the more glory comes to God when the answer comes.

   The reverse is also true. You will have as little as you are satisfied with. It's a tragic fact. The gospel of Luke 11:9–13 urges us to knock, seek, and ask. Some people are satisfied just to eke out a living. They want only a bare minimum.

They somehow think that's all they deserve. Not at all! Keep knocking, keep asking, keep seeking. God has much more to give. God commands it.

- ***You have as much of God as you have really wanted up to this point***. Paul Cain put it succinctly, "You are as close to Jesus as you want to be." The brother of Jesus gives us this promise, *"Draw near to God and He will draw near to you"* (James 4:8). Jesus told us in the Sermon on the Mount, *"Blessed are those who hunger and thirst after righteousness, for they shall be filled"* (Matthew 5:6).

Entering into rest

Jesus said, *"Come to Me, all you who labor and are heavy laden* [you who are exhausted], *and I will give you rest. Take My yoke upon you ... and you will find rest for your souls"* (Matthew 11:28–29). When you surrender your burdens to Jesus, the Holy Spirit comes in and gives you rest, and Jesus is honored.

Hebrews tells us, *"Today if you will hear His voice, do not harden your hearts ..."* (Hebrews 3:7–8) and further it says, talking about those who erred and did not regard the ways of God from Psalm 95, *"They shall not enter My rest"* (Hebrews 3:11). These people were disobedient. They didn't obey the voice of God's Spirit when He told them to enter and possess the land of promise. Are you aware that there is a prophetic parallel here? In their case, the Old Testament saints here had a land of promise. They journeyed all those years, yet they didn't enter in. In your case, you have prophetic promises that you are called to enter into.

It's possible for you not to enter into your place of destiny. God has a place for you, a place of promise and a place of destiny, but it is possible for you to miss it because of disobedience, because of not listening to the voice of God. What is God speaking to you?

Look again at what it says in Hebrews 4:7, *"Today, if you will hear His voice, do not harden your hearts."* Isn't it interesting that many are saying, "Oh, I'd love for the Lord to speak to me. I'd love to hear His voice." Would you really? According to this, the

Lord is speaking each and every day: through the Scriptures; through His Spirit; through circumstances; through others.

Paul asks, *"There are, it may be, so many kinds of languages in the world, and none of them is without significance"* (1 Corinthians 14:10). Youthful ideals, careers, education, adventure, travel, leadership, all these voices cry for attention. The writer to the Hebrews builds the entire epistle until he comes to the pinnacle of his message, *"See that you do not refuse Him who speaks"* (Hebrews 12:25). Your soul needs to lay it down. Your soul needs to give it a rest. Only then can you hear Him who is speaking.

There remains therefore a rest for the people of God, a rest for your soul. God's yoke is easy; yours is heavy (Matthew 11:28–30). Carrying yours around all day will, in fact, exhaust you. The Holy Spirit has no intention of endorsing such needs-driven behavior. We are, simultaneously, Spirit-led and needs-driven. The Bible tells us our hearts are desperately wicked and we don't even know it. We don't see our own needs-driven behavior which militates against God's rest. We need insight.

Marc Brisbois writes:

> My first real insight into my own "heart matters" came in the spring of 1982, while attending Christ for the Nations in Dallas, Texas. It was my first semester and I had been serving the Lord less than a year. My pursuit of the Lord had brought me repeatedly to the love chapter in 1 Corinthians 13 which reads:
>
> > *"Love suffers long and is kind; love does not envy; love does not parade itself, is not puffed up; does not behave rudely, does not seek its own, is not provoked, thinks no evil; does not rejoice in iniquity, but rejoices in the truth."*
> >
> > (1 Corinthians 13:4–6)
>
> I had become very familiar with these passages and the remainder of the chapter. Since it was my goal to become loving, I applied myself to practicing these principles as best I could. In my mind I was doing a fine job of living up to biblical "requirements". Despite my sincerity I was deceived.

And as most who are deceived, I did not know it – that is the nature of being deceived, you are unaware. Thankfully I was about to be delivered from my ignorance. I was about to receive a greater measure of the truth that would set me free.

Going under the knife

For months I had been praying in the spirit for profound change to come to my life. But I never really understood why until this day. With stunning clarity the Holy Spirit welded the Word of God into my heart. As I read these same Corinthians passages I had become so familiar with, it became the Sword of the Spirit. The purity of the love of God began to unfold before me with each verse I read. I began beholding the glory of God in the face of Jesus (2 Corinthians 3:18). It did two things: First it revealed how pure and true was the love of God. Secondly, as a direct and immediate effect of that revelation I saw the self-serving motivations of my heart. Words cannot adequately convey the shock of those brief, but seemingly endless moments.

The outer veneer of my good works began to peel back, exposing hidden ambitions. What was previously a kind gesture to a fellow student stood open and exposed before the revelation of the Sword of the Spirit. Hidden behind was a calculated effort to impress others; the need to convince myself I was a candidate for a great ministry; and desire to excel above others. The various implications of what I saw were numerous. I was deeply stunned! As I continued to read the passages, the level of conviction continued to increase. Tears began to roll down my cheeks as surprise gave way to horror. The depth of my heart's deceptive powers matched those of the most malevolent creatures I had seen depicted in movies and history. "How could this be?" I asked myself.

Continuing to read, it seemed as though every fiber of my being was a lie. Like Isaiah I thought, *"Woe is me, for I am undone! Because I am a man of unclean lips, and I dwell in the midst of a people of unclean lips; for my eyes have seen the King,* the LORD *of hosts"* (Isaiah 6:5). So bright was this glory it seemed to leave no stone unturned. Images of my daily lifestyle began to filter through my mind as I read down through the verses. When I came to the passage which said "love does not parade itself", I immediately saw myself dancing in chapel times. What I thought had been to the Lord suddenly became part of the elaborate attempt to appear spiritual. Possessing only a grain of true worship the majority of my attention was toward the student body. I had been performing for onlookers! Esteeming myself "set apart", a "true member" of an elite core of worshippers, I believed my dancing to be evidence of a superior dedication to which others should aspire. As the pride of my heart was being exposed the sense of repulsion I felt for myself made me want to hide. But where could I go?

When it seemed I would soon be crushed under the awesome weight of what seemed to be "cruel truth", the experience took a dramatic turn for the worse. I saw the open hands of Jesus holding what seemed to be an ugly mass of pure filth. So vivid was the vision I turned my head at the sight and smell. Unable to determine its form I asked the Lord what it was. He replied almost casually, "This is your heart". As painful as everything had been to that moment this seemed like a deathblow, which I could not endure. My thoughts turned like a whirlwind as I exited the room. Running across the courtyard I made my way to the prayer room above the cafeteria where I collapsed inches from the doorway.

My entire world seemed to be shaken as I lay sobbing. A combination of embarrassment, shame, shock, and disqualification flooded my being. Suddenly from the far side of the room a voice rang out in prophecy. It was another student who had been there quietly praying, unaware of what was happening to me. The words were both commending and accepting as the Father assured me of my place in His house and His love for me. Shame turned to comfort as in the shadow of some discipline His unchanging love shone through.

The fruit of revelation

The fruit of this encounter with the Lord is both great and varied. Above all of the perceptions gained, an awareness of the deceptiveness of the heart remains the most critical. If my own heart was selfish and deceptive, how could it be trusted to give my mind pure insights? The answer was clear: Man is incapable of objective judgment. Without the light of Christ's truth piercing through the darkness of our lives, we will always misinterpret what we see. It is the proverbial issue we so often see in the media today regarding the police department and issues of misconduct by them. Who polices the police? Can the police be trusted to properly judge themselves?

The heart of man is deceitfully wicked and unable to accurately judge itself. Infected by self-interest it cannot be objective. In as much as we cannot physically lift ourselves into the air, we cannot distance ourselves from the motives of the heart. This holds true whether or not you are a believer. Coming to Christ is the beginning of change, not the consummation. But since the heart holds a position of power it uses that power to insulate itself from change. It goes to great lengths to weave an elaborate trail of deception, permitting superficial acts of goodness, which serve only to mask greater depths of wickedness. What then is the answer to this human dilemma? The answer is simple. It is found in the humility which turns us to the Lord at the revelation of our hopeless condition. Our only hope is to hunger and thirst for the Truth, realizing we remain blind if we think we already see. (John 9:41)

Now, turn back to Hebrews 4 and we'll see this process God wants to take us though. Verse 10 says, *"He who has entered His rest has himself also ceased from his works as God did from His."* Like my friend Marc, your soul will find no rest if you keep on resisting the sanctification process, the weaning away from needs-driven-ness, or being needs-driven, to being Spirit-led.

Many of us remain at a shallow level of sanctification instead of progressing from one level to another to another. We need to constantly allow God's Word to pierce our hearts and change us. God's Word is able to divide "between joint and marrow" – flesh and spirit. That is, between needs-driven and Spirit-led. God's Word discerns the thoughts and intents of the heart. And as it happened with Marc, your motives are exposed. Are they needs-driven or are they Spirit-led?

The soul isn't, of itself, evil. The problem is that it has debris. It has wounds. It has a need to succeed or to receive acclaim. It needs to be thought well of. It needs to achieve greatness. It needs to prove itself. But this striving, restless thing we call a soul doesn't need annihilation. It needs to be sanctified.

Whose glory is it?

Paul said in 1 Corinthians chapter 3 that fire would consume all wood, hay and stubble – every work we have done that was not accomplished in the Spirit. To get beyond the wood and hay of the spiritual realm you are going to have to get deeper in Christ.

Jesus is soon coming for a beautiful bride. God is about to reveal Himself. This revelation will include the lost getting saved, the Church being renewed, healings, the miraculous (signs and wonders), a transfer of wealth. And it's all leading to something far more glorious than even that. The time has come for the Father to honor His Son.[2]

It is a season. We have entered that season. We are about to touch the glory and we have to understand what is about to take place. There is a corporate presence of the Lord coming. It's coming out of a supernatural place of rest. When He comes He demands worship. Even if you are a heathen, a Satanist, or an agnostic, when He comes you will bow. Your knee will bend.

A Muslim woman, a medical doctor, approached a friend of mine who is, himself, a doctor. The woman said to him, "I must know if Jesus is real." My friend told her to go home, ask and wait, and that Jesus would answer her. So she did. She went home, got in an empty room, asked the question and then waited.

The next day she reported back to my friend what happened. "After a period of silence and waiting," she told him, "a presence came into the room. I didn't know what it was or who it was. All I could do was worship. I was unable to stop myself. I couldn't stand. In that room, I was on my face. I just worshipped. I didn't dare even look up. After a while a voice spoke, saying, 'Now look at me.' I peeked up. It was a man in a brilliant, white robe. He was weeping. I screwed up my courage and asked, 'Why are you weeping?' 'These tears are for you,' he replied."

That same woman doctor was radically transformed on that day.

The following verse brings more enlightenment, *"Enter into the rock, and hide in the dust, from the terror of the* LORD *and glory of His majesty"* (Isaiah 2:10). We don't readily understand terror and majesty existing side-by-side. We think of terror as God's judgment and fierce anger, and majesty as glory and beauty and beneficence. And yet we can't have the majesty without the terror: *"Consider the goodness and severity of God"* (Romans 11:22).

In our society, we don't handle this sort of paradox very well. Yet, this terror and majesty side by side is the character of God. It's not just an issue of judgment *or* blessing – the one or the other – it is the government of God. That is what the Lord is about to bring back to His Church. The love relationship, the sense of identity, the bridal season we are entering; it is not a luxury. You will not be able to survive unless you know His heart for you.

Notes

1. The author wishes to acknowledge the contribution in this chapter from Christ for the Nations Institute, P.O. Box 769000, Dallas TX 75376–9000, particularly the categories of Future, Present and Maybe Blessings.
2. Acknowledgements to David Damien for his thoughts on God's end-time purposes and His presence and holiness in the last days. David Damien heads up Watchmen for the Nations and is located in Vancouver, B.C., Canada.

Chapter 7

Grace Enables Faith

The Bible says,

> *"For by grace you have been saved through faith, and that not of yourselves, it is the gift of God, not of works, lest anyone should boast."*
> (Ephesians 2:8–9)

We are saved by God's grace, and yet not all Christians understand grace. Often grace is defined as "unmerited favor". I would suggest this is an inadequate definition. In fact, it's more a definition of mercy. A more complete definition of grace would be: God's mighty, enabling power, freely given. Any time you see the word "grace" in the New Testament, substitute this definition and you will see how appropriate it really is.

Consider Ephesians 2:8 again: "For it is by *God's mighty, enabling power, freely given,* that you have been saved, through faith ..."

Or 1 Timothy 1:2 (NIV): *"Grace, mercy and peace from God the Father and Christ Jesus our Lord"* which then becomes, *"God's mighty, enabling power, freely given,* mercy and peace from God the Father and Jesus Christ our Lord."

Hebrews 13:9 (NIV) says,

> *"Do not be carried away by all kinds of strange teachings. It is good for our hearts to be strengthened by grace, not by ceremonial foods, which are of no value to those who eat them."*

In other words, it is not beneficial to try to establish your heart on any other foundation than grace.

The *establishing* and the *strengthening* of the heart by grace is a very powerful thing. It is, in fact, the difference between being stable and unstable in all your Christian life. Why can't people heal the sick or cast out demons consistently, for instance? God is the same yesterday, today and forever, after all. So, what's different? It is often because peoples' hearts aren't established, they aren't stable. This verse on strange teachings reminds me of what Paul said as he described unstable people. He referred to them as being "carried away" by every wind of teaching. All teaching, even good teaching (good words on healing, for example, or deliverance or miracles or spiritual warfare) will destabilize you if it is not firmly based on the grace of God.

I recall a story about a friend of mine called Jim. Jim pastored a church of more than two thousand people. It was a faith-filled, worshipping apostolic group of believers. For many years, the body had been thriving. But one day, Jim became seriously ill. His church fasted and prayed, expecting God to heal him. He didn't improve. Instead, he was hospitalized. His illness continued for months. Gradually, family by family, people left the church, declaring they had no pastor. He was hospitalized and they didn't know if he would ever improve. Finally, the church had to close down. There was no one left. Jim was extremely desperate and discouraged by now. Still he sunk lower and lower until he was hovering between life and death. At this extreme moment, at the point of death, God spoke to him: "Jim, I want you to forget everything you ever learned about healing. I want you to know this one thing. Healing is my love." Immediately God healed him and raised him up – restored – and God gave him back a church of four thousand people.

Who's a genius, anyway?

Time and again I have seen people deliver complex and impenetrable teaching on healing. People have written volumes laying out the most complex conditions, rules and regulations about the ministry of healing, so that you would have to be a rocket scientist to understand it all and to minister or to receive healing. Wow! That leaves me out. And probably a few of you, as well.

When I see such teachings I wonder if it could be that these people have somehow lost sight of the simplicity that is in Christ? The subtlety of legalism offers some fascinating insights. *"I fear,"* Paul said, *"... lest ... your minds may be corrupted from the simplicity that is in Christ"* (2 Corinthians 11:3). The great revelation of the gospel is simplicity. God is for people. God wants to lift people out of misery and hopelessness and defeat grinding poverty and sickness. God says that great grace is available to you today in order to minister that to a hurt world. This gospel is really good news. Good news to the many people living lives of quiet desperation.

One man was admitted to a mental hospital. He received 40 shock treatments and was a virtual vegetable. He had had a homosexual lifestyle and a fourth grade education. People were faithful to bring him the grace of God. They witnessed to him. God healed him and raised him up. Today he is a pastor, happy, whole, with a wife and three lovely daughters. One day he asked Jesus, "Lord, I am a recipient of Your magnificent grace. Please show me more." Suddenly he had a vision. A hand reached down and picked him up by the nape of the neck and immersed him in an ocean stretching as far as the eye could see. The hand then lifted him out. He was soaking, dripping wet. "See the water dripping from your body?" the Lord said to him. "That is the amount of my grace you have received thus far in your life. Now look at the ocean. That is the amount of my grace that is still available to you this side of eternity."

Ephesians 3:17 states that we are, *"rooted and grounded in love."* The Father loves us passionately. The love of God is shed abroad in our hearts by the Holy Spirit (Romans 5:5). It dominates us. We love because He first loved us.

A hymn writer of old wrote:

Were the whole realm of nature mine,
That were an offering far too small.
Love so amazing, so divine
Demands my soul, my life, my all.

There is a grace that demands the seizing, the laying hold of. Does that grace give us license to sin? Paul posed the same question two thousand years ago (Romans 6:1). And the answer is still the same. Of course not! The grace of God teaches us not to sin. The grace of God is an instructor.

The law is also an instructor. My righteousness is not based on what I do. Whew! God is, indeed, merciful to me. It's based on what Jesus did and that will change what I do. That's the key. One of the great freedoms in Christianity, often cited, is the freedom to be wrong. But the greatest freedom is the freedom to do right.

Happiness is . . .

Did you know that there are people in this world, unbelievers, non-Christians, who are happier than a great many Christians? How so, you might ask. It's because they aren't suffering from guilt and condemnation from trusting in the law and, at the same time, trying to appropriate grace. What an amazing thing. Jesus told us to watch out for the leaven of the Pharisees. Paul tells us that a little leaven leavens the whole lump. In other words, just a little legalism goes a long way to producing hypocrisy.

God can't use a legalistic heart. All healing, all of God's miraculous power, comes through hearts that are established and settled in grace, not through legalistic hearts. James says, "A double-minded man is unstable in all of his ways" (James 1:8). Another way to say that would be double-covenanted, i.e., one who is slipping back and forth between law and grace. James tells us, *"Let not that man suppose that he will receive anything from the Lord"* (James 1:7). I believe this is crucial. For those of you who want to experience healing, settle your hearts, establish your hearts. Let your hearts be rooted firmly in the grace of God, the "enablement" of God.

James further tells us, in chapter 4:8, *"Purify your hearts, you double-minded* [double-covenanted]*."* Some of the most unstable people in the world are not the prostitutes, pimps and drug dealers. They're steady and they do a steady business. Rather it is believers who fail to grasp the depths of God's grace! There are way too many Christians in mental institutions.

Now, here's the hope for you. If a double-minded person can't receive anything, then the opposite must be true as well. A single-minded person can receive much, even miracles. Single-minded means single-covenanted. It means your heart is settled, your mind is settled, on grace.

So again I say: focus your life; focus your heart; be single-minded. The mind is a reproductive area. If you focus on grace, you reproduce grace and life. If you focus on the law, you reproduce the law and death.

God's amazing grace

> *"Immediately the girl arose and walked, for she was twelve years of age. They were overcome with great amazement."*

> (Mark 5:42)

I would like to share for your encouragement a report of some friends of mine, a testimony of God's grace poured out in healing power:

A Divine Visitation
by Linda Sutch and Anne Rasmussen
It was a Friday evening in Challis, Washington, October 21, 2002. Intercessors from various areas and members of the ministry team gathered from 2:00–5:00 p.m. prior to the first service. Upon entering the sanctuary, the presence of the Lord was already felt. The floor of the sanctuary in front of the altar shook (it felt like a continuous earthquake) and what appeared to be diamonds and gold dust appeared around the room. There was great anticipation. After a season of praise and worship Bob Brasset began ministering in teaching and the miraculous. As people were worshipping the Lord, the Holy Spirit began to touch them with the power of God and the healing began. Again, what appeared to be diamonds and gold dust and the fragrance of the Holy Spirit manifested in even greater abundance.

The fire falls

Then the fire fell. That's the only way this writer can describe it. The fire of God came into the room! People were burning up! Great heat ... people trying to fan themselves, describing it as burning, as fire, even as a "Baptism of Fire". Two sisters were immediately touched by that fire and power and went down prostrate with intensity of burning and electricity. The heat of the Holy Spirit then hit a young lady and she was healed of chronic pain in her left shoulder and arm. From that moment, the fire of God flowed throughout the auditorium and laughter in the Holy Ghost rippled and then exploded through the congregation. So much was happening. How to record it all? People weeping and sobbing, others laughing joyously, others repenting, all happening at once seemingly orchestrated by an invisible hand. The pastors of the local church, Bill & Connie Pinneo, were hit by the power of God and they were slain together in the Holy Spirit. A woman was then healed in her hands from arthritis as the power of God came upon her and a snapping sound was heard in her hands. A command was given for healing reconstruction of all bones, muscles and nerves to go into place in another woman's body. Immediately things snapped into place and she was healed from pain and problems in her shoulder and body and her fingers, which could not move or work separately, now they were instantly released to do so.

More glory

A charge of energy hit another woman on the side of her head and she was healed completely of back problems. The glory seemed to increase. One church pew began shaking, and continued to shake throughout the meeting. A woman in that pew who had sprained her left ankle right before the meeting and was in much pain, was hit by the power of God and began to jump on her ankle, completely healed. Her sister, who had a chronic heart disease, which manifested in blueness of face and extremities, because of shortness of breath, was given a brand new heart! Another man reported the next day a new heart after years of serious heart disease. The glory was given to God with shouts of much joy. The floor also increased its shaking in the front of the auditorium as the sovereign power of the Holy Spirit continued to move. The transference of anointing began flowing and hitting people as people were called forward and the fire or anointing would leap from one person to another. This is difficult to describe. How does one describe the indescribable? A man who was hit by the power of God remained on the floor for the next two hours, manifesting God's presence in a powerful way and was taken up into the heavenlies.

A woman who came forward for respiratory healing was also healed of a broken bone in the top of her foot as the fire of God came upon her. A word of knowledge went out and a woman was healed of right rotator cuff pain in her shoulder, as well as restoration to the cartilage. The stiffness was released and the inflammation disappeared. Pastor Bill Pinneo came for prayer for his left arm for tendonitis and both arms were healed. Sixteen people went forward for healing of asthma and allergies and were touched and healed by the power of God. One woman with allergies to grasses left the church and rubbed grass from outside the church around her eyes and nose to prove her healing, with no effect whatever of her former allergies. God recreated and began the restoration process of a man who had been a logger. He had chronic back pain in his spinal column for over 16 years from being hit by a car and a log. His pelvis was also healed and put in proper alignment and his arm was lengthened. As the congregation watched, he grew taller and his shoulders went into proper alignment. He also received healing in his heart for inherited heart disease and a lady in the congregation said that she saw a hole in his heart being healed.

An 82-year old woman who had been a beautician during her professional years was healed of stiffness and inflammation and chronic problems that resulted from her profession. A word of knowledge came to a woman of the congregation, after God used her in healing another woman, that she would train people in the gifts of healing. They would go to

the nations with the miraculous healing power of God –
even to seeing eyes put back into their sockets.

Incurable diseases healed

One came up who had had an incurable bronchial condition
for 15 years, which also had resulted in a staphylococcus
infection in her lungs. As she was prayed for she was
instantly healed. Truly this was an evening to remember.
This city has now experienced a genuine visitation! It is the
kind of thing you read about in the history of revivals. This
is only the first night. This is unto something. This is unto
the harvest. The fields are ripe! What totally struck us and
even flabbergasted us as we observed, sometimes with our
mouths open wide in wonderment, was the extreme variety
and power of manifestations! I know we are not supposed
to glorify manifestations but they sure let us know how
powerful, loving and real Jesus is!!!! After all isn't this what it
is all about? GLORIFYING OUR WONDERFUL JESUS?

God's mighty power

We really are living in days of God's mighty power. It's time we
dared to believe God. It's time we cast off luke-warmness and
apathy like a worn-out garment and allowed Jesus to clothe us
with His expectancy. The prophet Haggai proclaimed, *"The glory
of this latter temple shall be greater than the former"* (Haggai 2:9).
We need faith to recognize that any time the Word is preached,
God wants to confirm it with a demonstration of signs and
wonders as affirmed in the following two verses:

> *"And my speech and my preaching were not with persuasive
> words of human wisdom, but in demonstration of the Spirit and
> of power ... "*   (1 Corinthians 2:4)

and

> *" ... the Lord working with them and confirming the word
> through the accompanying signs."*   (Mark 16:20)

A day without miracles is a boring day. Daily we need to pray, "Amaze us, God. May we be in awe of you and your mighty power today, Lord." Do you read any instructions to the contrary in the Scriptures? For too long we've allowed man's puny accomplishments to amaze us (splitting the atom, rocketing to the moon, 73 home runs in a season etc.). It's time to be overawed by God Himself and Him only. *"He is awesome in His doing toward the sons of men"* (Psalm 66:5).

While natural works glorify man and have no lasting value, supernatural works glorify God. They often cause a ruckus, too! One day a man sick of palsy was brought to Jesus. Jesus immediately forgave the man's sins. Many of the crowd were shocked. Who did this man think he was, anyway? When Jesus saw their hearts, He turned his attention back to the sick man and healed him.

> *"Immediately* [the sick man] *arose, took up the bed, and went out in the presence of them all, so that all were amazed and glorified God, saying, 'We never saw anything like this!'"*
>
> (Mark 2:12)

The man's sins were forgiven. His body was healed. The crowd was now awed. And God got the glory. Isn't that exactly how it should work?

Chapter 8

Becoming Faith-Filled

You have a unique design. It's not something you had a lot of say in. It's the Holy Spirit's design. He has given you a special gift-mix and it is this gift-mix that uniquely qualifies you for a particular function in Jesus' body. Many Christians function outside of their gift-mix. This can work to a degree, but it's rather awkward. It requires great exertion. It's draining.

The designer, the Holy Spirit, desires that Christ in you is expressed through your soul to others. He wants to bring us into proper alignment. Instead of awkwardness, there can be a smooth flowing of the Holy Spirit's power in our lives. Instead of serving God being draining, there can be real peace. Instead of undue fatigue, there can be rest. The writer of Hebrews tells us, *"For we who have believed do enter that rest"* (Hebrews 4:3). This is anointed believing. You have an inward abiding anointing and it energizes your faith, and your faith in turn, brings rest to your soul.

Jesus told us that it is the ones who are childlike who are capable of this type of rest for their souls. In other words, these are the qualities that anoint faith:

- Childlike simplicity
- Honesty
- An open heart

Jesus put it this way in Matthew 11:25–27,

> *"I thank you Father, Lord of heaven and earth, that You have hidden these things from the wise and prudent and have revealed*

them to babes. Even so, Father, for so it seemed good in Your sight. All things have been delivered to Me by My Father, and no one knows the Son except the Father. Nor does anyone know the Father except the Son, and the one to whom the Son wills to reveal Him."

Here, Jesus expresses the value of childlike faith and then transitions from revelation and childlikeness to what the revelation actually gives us: Nor does anyone know the Father except the Son, and the one to whom the Son wills to reveal Him. No one knows who you are except the Holy Spirit. Who you really are is a mystery to you and to those around you until God opens your heart.

The Scriptures give us many pictures of this deep work of God. One of these found in Hebrews, which we've looked at before, helps us greatly in understanding the way in which God opens up our hearts:

"For the word of God is living and powerful, and sharper than any two-edged sword, piercing even to the division of soul and spirit, and of joints and marrow, and is a discerner of the thoughts and intents of the heart."   (Hebrews 4:12)

Just as the marrow is encased in the bone, the spirit of man is encased in the soul. The bone must be broken if the marrow, the inner essence, is to be released. And that's what the Word, the sword of the Spirit does for us. It reveals or releases the inner man. Jesus' outward man however, was in complete harmony with and subjugation to His inner man – His Spirit. Unlike any other human, ever, he didn't need the division. His flesh, though tempted, wasn't sinful. Remember that he had no natural father and so He inherited no sin. No breaking, no division between bone and marrow was necessary.

Get the order right

To release God's Spirit and His anointing in our lives, a breaking of self-will must occur in us. It is an "opening of our heart".

The apostle Paul put it this way: *"The Spirit searches all things, yes, the deep things of God"* (1 Corinthians 2:10). There are things inside of you that your conscious mind knows little or nothing about. These things are deeper than the faculties of memory or reason or imagination. But the Holy Spirit knows all about you and He searches all things and every part of you. He knows exactly how the Father sees you and what plans the Father has for you.

Our fleshly man is busy considering outward appearance, how we appear and how our actions and reactions appear before man. The Bible tells us to go deeper. It instructs us to consider, through His word and His Spirit, and to examine our hearts. The Gospel is a heart Gospel. It's not a Gospel in which performance produces power. It's a Gospel where power produces performance! Get it? The cross of Christ is the power of God, but it is also an offence, a reproach. Why? Because it gives God's righteousness and promises and holiness to heathens! They didn't become righteous because they stopped their idolatry, their perversions and their filthy practices. They became righteous in order that they would be able (have the power, the means) to stop the idolatry, perversions and filthy practices. Again, the order here is essential.

There is no formula for having your heart healed. It is merely the fact that Jesus came to heal the broken hearted and to reconcile the heathen unto Himself (2 Corinthians 5:19). This glorious Gospel we proclaim reveals that a person can have God's righteousness not through works. As Martin Luther discovered, *"The just shall live by faith"* (Hebrews 10:38).

Paul says it is possible to fall from that grace. He's not speaking about losing our salvation. He's telling us that it's possible to fall from living in God's favor, grace and power. Four basic things happen when Christians fall from living in God's grace:

1. The heart breaks.
2. The individual falls under condemnation.
3. The Christian then operates under the law of condemnation and self-inflicted punishment.
4. The soul seeks out an escape from the pain.

This escape from pain is a bandage, a substitute for true intimacy, faith and grace, and it happens along these lines: false spirituality, illicit sexual expression, occult and witchcraft involvement, addictions and drug misuse, undue emphasis on wealth and material goods.

Gentle anger

Most Christians are living with a pre-programmed "scripting" in their soul and this scripting holds us back from fully hearing God and exercising faith. The power to minister effectively is thus greatly diminished or even non-existent. Each Christian needs a revelation and an experience of the Father's heart.

Paul tells us in Romans 5:5, *"The love of God has been poured out in our hearts by the Holy Spirit who was given to us."* He's saying that it takes the supernatural enablement and empowering of the Holy Spirit for us to experience the felt affection and love of the Father. Most Christians don't experience that love in any appreciable measure. How can you tell? Try asking the question: "Does God love you?" Then listen closely to the answers. People will probably say something like, "Yes, God loves me and Jesus died for my sins." They may even quote scriptures about God's love. But when the same people are probed as to what they actually feel and experience, other things will come out:

1. God is angry with them.
2. God is disappointed with them (sort of a gentle anger).
3. God doesn't like them.
4. God doesn't favor them or regard them very highly.

Such gloomy, negative thoughts often block the great, abundant supply God has to give us. Such things as:

1. A love for His Son.
2. His felt affection in our hearts.
3. An enablement and equipping in supernatural ministry.

These positive elements are often completely absent from a Christian's experience. Or, when they're found, they're unstable and diminished. Now Satan knows this and out of these facts he has developed a six-thousand-year-old strategy of containment and damage control. One of the ways he releases this plan is to have Christians pre-occupied with self. In the Church we have a self-help obsession. If you read a list of best sellers in a Christian bookstore, what do you find? There are many titles covering the following topics:

1. Self-worth
2. Self-esteem
3. Self-help
4. Self-motivation
5. Self-promotion

Did someone mention the word 'self' here somewhere?!

Just k.i.s.s.

Don't get me wrong, now. There really is a place in the Church for true, biblical counseling. I've done much of it, myself, in my own ministry. And there are plenty of inspiring, good Christian books of the ilk mentioned above. But there exists, too, a counterfeit, and this counterfeit seeks to replace the Gospel in the Church. It's a brand of psychology that no longer calls Adam and Eve the first sinners but, instead, the first dysfunctional family. Problems like low self-esteem, poor self-image, insecurity and feelings of inadequacy all take the focus away from the cross and on to self. They replace sin, pride, lust, love of money and envy and the like. It all gets arrayed in supposedly more palatable non-biblical language. We're getting another Gospel. Keep it simple, stupid, as someone abruptly but aptly put it. The simplicity of the Gospel. Never stray far from it. Not in your worship, not in your dealing with the world, not in your musings and reflections. Not anytime.

I.D. please

When we have a true sense of our identity in Christ, then a true sense of our great value and worth comes forth. At the Jordan

River, God the Father spoke publicly over the Son: *"This is My beloved Son, in whom I am well pleased"* (Matthew 3:17). This was before Jesus had done any public ministry and His Father was affirming Him. Today God wants to do His mighty works through sons and daughters all over the world who know their true identity.

One of my favorite healing miracles concerns a little seven-year-old boy. The setting was a renewal-style meeting. The little boy came forward for prayer again and again, perhaps seven or eight times in total. Each time the power of God would touch him and he would fall backwards and rest peacefully in the spirit for perhaps 15 minutes. He'd then jump up, play for a few minutes, then go back for more prayer. His mother watched all this.

Eventually she became concerned. She approached her boy finally, and asked him why he kept going back for prayer again and again. It wasn't a game, she told him. The little boy replied, "I know it isn't a game but every time I go up there and they pray over me, something touches me. It feels good. Then I am lying on the floor. I can't stand up right away. Every time I lie there I see Jesus. He keeps telling me, 'You are mine. You belong to me.' It feels so good, Mommy." That same boy had been abused by his first grade teacher.

Through all that God is doing today, through the anointed faith and through healing and renewal, there is a voice that keeps coming back, over and over, "You are my beloved son. You are my beloved daughter." It's the heart of God. Through all the healings, and all the miracles, God keeps telling us that we please Him. Because of His Son, He is so pleased with us.

Throughout Church history, there have been many movements, many outpourings of revival and renewal. Each of these outpourings has brought with it a renewed emphasis on a particular truth. For example, the power of the Spirit, or an emphasis on worship, or an emphasis on the Bible as the Word of God. Other movements have centered around the importance of water baptism, or spiritual warfare, or the priesthood of all believers, or divine healing. The one truth that has never, until this current outpouring, broken through to the Church as a whole is this: His Heart as Father. God wants to bring peace to the soul of the Church. He wants to continue to bring a revelation of the Father's heart to the Church.

We have a corporate lack of identity in the Church. We can easily discern this by the symptoms it produces. Consider the following questions:

- How susceptible are we to fads in the Church?
- How vulnerable are we to church population drift?
- How prone are we to sensationalism and pre-eminence?

Our identity doesn't come from possessions. Nor is it to be found in achievement. Our identity comes from belonging. Jesus doesn't say, "Well done, good and successful servant," He says, instead, *"Well done good and faithful servant"* (Matthew 25:21). The issue is what can God entrust to us? If the answer is just a little, that's okay. If we are faithful in a little He will entrust more to us. And so it will grow.

Jesus chose to live among us for 33 years. Why? It was His love, His complete identification with you and me. Then, in the last $3\frac{1}{2}$ in His public ministry, He gave us His perspective on leadership, ministry and on how a person develops in the Kingdom. There is a growth and development in the Kingdom. We do not become super saints at the instant of salvation. We are instantly saved, yes, we are translated from darkness to light at the moment of the new birth. But there follows a lifetime (however long that be) of change. A lifetime of exercising faith and growing.

I am going to be greatly occupied by the quest for knowing Jesus (discovering my identity) for the rest of my life. Ministry is not what is going to occupy all my time and energy. Yes, it will take up a large portion, but not as much as it used to. Instead it's ministry to Him that is important! That's the ministry I'm after. Each of us is a priest. Priests offer spiritual sacrifices. I want to know how to lift up holy hands in the holiest place, the secret place of the most high (Psalm 91). And I want to be a blessing to my Father's heart.

In Ezekiel, the priests are told not to wear any woolen garments. The reason might surprise you. Wool produces sweat and sweat stinks. But the critical element is this: sweat represents human effort as it keeps trying to produce God's works.

Internet plea

Shawna lived in Chicago. She was a street prostitute and a drug addict for 20 years. Cirrhosis of the liver, crack and cocaine addiction, hepatitis C virus, all combined to put her life in peril. The doctors said she wouldn't live much longer. One day Jesus sovereignly began revealing Himself to her in a series of amazing visions. Shawna was both amazed and confused. Not having any formal connection with God or religion or the Church, she sought out several pastors to explain what was happening to her. The ministers she spoke to were unable or unwilling to help her, for whatever reasons. She thought she was going insane. As a last gasp effort, she put out a plea on the internet.

"Can someone help me? I think I'm going mad. Here is what has been happening to me. I'm a hopeless case. Can anyone understand or help?" She went on to explain about the visions.

A Christian lady in Seattle replied, "Yes, I understand. Jesus is revealing Himself to you and wants to save and heal you. If you will get on a plane and fly out to the West Coast, I'll meet you and bring you to a healing meeting and there Jesus will heal and save you." Shawna responded and came to Seattle. The meeting was one that my wife Sue and I were ministering at. We called Shawna forward at the meeting and began ministering healing. My wife Sue laid hands on her. Shawna explains the rest of the story in her own words:

> I was such a desperate woman. I had no one to turn to and I booked a flight to Seattle on the strength of an email that I received from a woman I didn't even know. That's how desperate I felt. But God was so faithful. I realize now it was He who was prompting me. When I got on the phone, my body became hot. I was burning up. (I realize now this was God's presence and power touching my body. It was like fire.) This burning continued throughout the whole journey from Chicago to Seattle and back again.

When Bob called me forward, the heat on my body increased. Then Sue laid her hands on me. The power increased even more and the area over my liver began vibrating rapidly. After about 5 minutes of this, people observing me began gasping. "Her complexion (yellow and jaundiced from liver diseased, etc.) is changing." It truly did. It changed to a normal, rosy, healthy hue, as people watched.

Jesus healed me, saved me and set me free that night. But that wasn't all. The power and the heat and the anointing continued on my body all the way back to Chicago. When I arrived back in Chicago and took a taxi to my home, something happened. I opened the door to the house we were living in and the power of God hit the building. Two other people were in the house at the time and they fell out under the power and lay there prostrate, unable to move for four hours. Jesus is so wonderful!

Chapter 9

Mystery

What if I tell you that living by faith could become as easy as breathing? What if I were to tell you that with a simple adjustment of focus you could turn your faith into an explosion of God's power and love that would be life-changing for you?

Let me take you on a journey. In this journey, I'll show you a path that puts Jesus as the central focus of your faith's gaze. It's a path that puts the cross of Christ as the source of your power. And a true spirit of witness (the Greek meaning literally, "martyrdom") as your heart attitude. I am going to share a scriptural revelation that millions have missed. It's the secret of resurrection power.

In Ephesians chapter 1, Paul prayed that the Church would have the wisdom to accept revelation about our unique position in Jesus. Paul went on to say that he wanted us to grasp, *". . . what are the riches of the glory of His inheritance in the saints"* (verse 18). Jesus inherited something. It's rich, it's glorious and it's from the Father. Jesus inherited the right to live in us and express Himself fully through us. It is a glorious mystery! Paul calls it, *"Christ in you, the hope of glory"* (Colossians 1:27).

Identification

This is the glorious truth of *identification*. Jesus so identified with us that He became one of us. He so identified with us that He said, in effect, "Father, they deserve death and eternal damnation. I'll take their place in punishment so that they can take a place in favor with you." This is the glory, the mystery and the power of identification.

> *"God was in Christ reconciling the world to Himself, not imputing their trespasses to them."* (2 Corinthians 5:19)

There is nothing in the heart of God that *wants* to find fault with us. But neither is there anything in the character of God that can allow Him to overlook our sin. So because we're pretty filthy and He longs to draw us near, He put all our filth on His Son. Through Him we're righteous. Not a righteousness born of perfect performance and conduct. That would be something we could – everyone could – applaud. But the righteousness, the record of perfect conduct and obedience, and the credit, all belongs to Jesus. It is the perfect conduct of God's own Son.

My normal condition, then, is knowing that I am loved, knowing that I am forgiven, knowing that I am cleansed, knowing that I am sanctified. God likes me. He enjoys me, even in my immaturity and imperfection. That's just the way it is. And in my spirit I respond joyously to Him. But if I move out of that position of knowing who I am in Christ, I come to an unrest, a troubled attitude, a disquiet in my spirit.

Identification is the backbone of Paul's theology. He said, in effect, the anointed one, the Messiah, is not just Jesus. We are the body of God's Messiah and Jesus is the head. He so identifies with us that Jesus told Paul when he was still known as Saul that when he persecuted Christians he persecuted Him (Acts 9:4).

Mystery solved

But can living by faith be as easy or natural as breathing? I breathe because it's my nature to breathe. I do it without thinking. I do it when I'm asleep. Not so living by faith. It's something else. Something greater than me. Something to be constantly struggled toward. Well, isn't it?

Paul went on to say that Christ's crucifixion was our crucifixion (Galatians 2:20). His burial was our burial. His resurrection and ascension was our resurrection and ascension. His reward our reward. After all, everything that happens to the head happens to the body. When the Son of Man conquered sickness and death, we conquered sickness and death (through Him). Jesus' very nature is as an overcomer. Eureka! That's it.

We are overcomers because it's in us to be overcomers. Just as it's in our lungs to continue to draw air even while we sleep. That's what makes them lungs. We are overcomers, not because we've done any deed that would merit the title, but because we're Christians, part of the body of Christ. We live by faith and walk in obedience because that's the nature of Christ, our Head. We are the body of Christ. We have the nature of Christ. This revelation of identification is a powerful truth. It will revolutionize our focus and our faith if we let it.

Paul says to the Church at Rome, *"For if by the one man's offense death reigned through the one ..."* (Romans 5:17). The whole human race, Jew and Gentile, all of man with his sin, was judged on the cross. There was a "corporate" man on the cross. The Adamic race was crucified there. That's what Paul tells us. *"For as in Adam all die, even so in Christ,* [the last Adam] *all shall be made alive"* (1 Corinthians 15:22). Jesus became the *last* Adam. There is no second Adam. He was the last Adam because all the judgment of Adam ended in Him. There really is no more to be done.

An eternal moment

Jesus took to Himself, to His bosom, all the peoples of all time. He embraced us. It was a moment out of time. It reached into the future and into the past. It embraced, Paul tells us, Jew and Gentile alike (Romans 1:16). That means that Billy Graham and Adolf Hitler, Pope John Paul and Paul the apostle, Tiger Woods and Woodrow Wilson, Saddam Hussein and Mother Teresa, and you and me. If we will but believe, the riches of Christ will be ours. The reason? So that in Jesus, God might create one new man: Jesus the Messiah, head and body.

That's the mystery of the Gospel. It's the fact that there are only two men on the planet – Adam and Christ. You are either in one or in the other. One body, Adam, has already been judged and will go into that judgment. Those in Adam refuse to repent. They refuse to believe. They refuse to trust. And they will not live. They will not set one foot in heaven.

But for those who will believe and receive and repent and trust, oh the glory! Adam's debt has already been paid in full. For all who have ears to hear, that is very good news. That's the Gospel. All sin, all sickness has already been atoned for.

Thus, there is a threefold purpose to our lives in Christ here on earth:

1. We are to spread the good news. That means we are to announce it, preach it, proclaim it and live it.
2. We are to heal the sick and to cast out demons. Remember that He Who is in you is greater than he who is in the world.
3. We're to win the lost for Christ.

Kingdom advancers

If a willing person could get close enough to Jesus while He was on earth, that person received the ministry of the Kingdom, i.e. healing, cleansing, forgiveness of sins. That's the purpose of Jesus' body today. Anyone who gets close enough to us is supposed to get the ministry of the Kingdom: healing, cleansing and forgiveness. The power has not diminished, nor has it changed.

In God's Divine wisdom and fore-knowledge, He prepared three bodies for His Son. At Bethlehem, He gave Jesus a body that would die. On Resurrection Sunday, He gave Jesus a body that was immortal and glorious and would live forever. At Pentecost, He gave Jesus a body that would function. That's us. We're now commissioned to function as an expression of Jesus on the earth. The resurrection of our Messiah from the dead was the defining moment of all reality. It's the foundation on which all our faith rests.

There are five steps whereby we identify with Christ:

1. ***We went with Him to the cross.*** *"I have been crucified with Christ"* (Galatians 2:20).

There needs to be a real expression and a personal knowledge of the Son of God in our lives. George Whitfield was a marvelous revivalist, soul winner and preacher of the Gospel. One day two contemporaries were discussing his ministry. One said, "George Whitfield, to accomplish all that he is doing in winning many tens of thousands to Christ, must be powerfully gifted." The other man wisely replied, "It's not that George is so powerfully gifted and anointed. He's powerfully crucified!"

2. **We died with Him**. When He died, two thousand years ago, we died too. It is an actual historic fact. Whether we know it or not, whether we believe it or not, it did happen. *"For the love of Christ compels us, because we judge thus: that if One died for all, then all died"* (2 Corinthians 5:14).

Mind you, the flesh wants to live. And as long as it is alive it will struggle to do its fleshly, sinful acts. But the cross ever looms as a death sentence, to all flesh, to all personal pride, to lust and to selfish ambition.

3. **We were buried with Him**. This is the backbone of Paul's theology. Did you know that this identification is actually a two-way street? Christ identified with us. He paid our penalty. He is in us. And we identify with Him – in death, in life. He is the vine. We are the branches (John 15).

This identification is so powerful that you can stand in faith, on your baptism in water (the sign of your burial with Him) to break the power of any sin or sin habit in your life. Why? Because when you're baptized you publicly declare your identification with Christ. This is so important.

If I might be permitted an aside, for a picture of baptism, imagine a crowd of people standing in a field when an earthquake strikes and the earth begins to split apart, dividing the crowd, as well. You are right there. You point to the other side. "I belong on that side," you say. "Those are my people and that is my ground." That means your fate is with whatever happens to the other side, whether the ground sinks into the abyss or not. Whatever happens. But it isn't real, it doesn't really happen, until you step across. Confession is the initial choice. Baptism is the step.

4. ***We were made alive***. Remember the scripture from earlier in the chapter? In Christ, all shall be made alive. He has made (past tense) us alive together with Him (1 Corinthians 15:22).

How did He make us alive when we were hopelessly lost in sin? And how is it that God imputed Adam's sin to us in the first place? You don't understand it fully? Me neither. But we don't have to have complete comprehension of everything. We just have to believe it and walk in it. The Bible tells us, *"By faith we understand . . . "* (Hebrews 11:3).

He did it by the law of identification and inheritance, and by federal headship. Adam was the federal head of the human race. We received his inheritance, all of it, both good and bad.

How do we get what Jesus got? By that same law of inheritance/identification and federal headship.

"We were buried with Him through baptism into death, that just as Christ was raised from the dead by the glory of the Father, even so we also should walk in newness of life."
(Romans 6:4)

5. ***We are seated with Him***. *"And God raised us up with Christ and seated us with him in the heavenly realms in Christ Jesus"* (Ephesians 2:6 NIV).

Being seated with Christ is to be in that place of rest whereby we cease from our own labors. It's the place of authority. Paul was probably the most hated man in hell because of this revelation. When people grasp this, when they apprehend this truth and begin practicing it, lives are transformed. Whole neighborhoods, whole ethnic groups, nations and societies are changed.

I didn't do it

One day a son, who was a very obedient young man, was in the garden talking to his father, when some men came to arrest him. Now they were rather rough and tumble fellows and he had done nothing wrong, but although he had his father and many friends around, he let the men take him away anyway. He remained silent as they proceeded to beat him. Then they hauled him into a courtroom and convicted him on some absurd charge or other and he didn't complain. Then, with whips and scourges they drove him, carrying a big, heavy piece of lumber, to the top of a small hill on the outskirts of town. There, they stripped him naked. And as he lay down they pounded two long, sharp spikes right through his hands and into the piece of lumber, pinning his arms to the wood. Then they drove another spike through his feet and into the wood, pinning them as well. This all happened on a Friday afternoon some years back. Then they raised the piece of lumber with him hanging on it. And as this young man, who was always obedient, hung from those nails, naked and agonizing and bleeding and dying, his father reached down, took some of the blood and with it sealed a covenant.

At the outset of this chapter, I said that your faith could be turned into an explosion of God's power and love. Our identification with Christ and the realization of His total, all-encompassing identification with us brings exactly that – a transformation of our faith. It is that transformation, that change, that enables us to experience the same resurrection power that Jesus experienced when the Father raised Him from the dead.

Chapter 10

Action God

"For in Christ Jesus
neither circumcision nor uncircumcision
avails anything, but faith working through love."
(Galatians 5:6)

The Greek word translated "working" in this verse is *energos*. It means empowered. The passage could actually be translated, "What really matters is faith that is empowered or energized or anointed by love." I said at the beginning of this book that true faith is "anointed believing". The anointing that comes on our faith and makes it powerful, active and enduring is the love anointing.

When the gospels describe Jesus healing people they never say, "Jesus was moved by faith", or "Jesus was moved by power". However, they do state many times, "Jesus was moved by love," or, "Jesus was moved by compassion." And Jesus didn't just feel this love or this compassion, it actually *moved* Him to *do something*. Love moved Him to action. The result? Again and again we hear, He gave people their sight; He gave people something to eat (loaves and fishes); He healed their diseases; He set them free from demons. In fact, the four gospels speak more about compassion (or love) than they do about faith.

The compassion that wells up in us is nothing like inert. It calls for, it demands a response. Compassion to action. A love God. An Action God. Smith Wigglesworth often reflected that compassion called forth a powerful faith response, as the following extract reveals:

An urgent call for help

During the early years of his ministry, Smith Wigglesworth received a desperate telegram from a family in a town some two hundred miles away, pleading with him to come pray for a young woman. Without hesitation, Wigglesworth travelled the distance as quickly as possible.

Upon his arrival, Wigglesworth discovered that a young woman had become a raging demoniac. Her parents and husband were distraught with the situation. They could not even bring the baby to her to nurse, for fear of the harm she might do to herself or the infant.

The family led Wigglesworth up a staircase to a room where the young mother was on the floor, being held down by five men. Even though she was physically very frail, the evil power that controlled her was more than a match for all five.

As Wigglesworth entered the room, the evil spirits that possessed her stared out of her eyes and snarled at him, "We are many. You can't cast us out."

With complete calm, Wigglesworth firmly stated, "Jesus can. Greater is He that is in me that he that is in the world."

"She's ours. We won't give her up!" the demonic voices growled repeatedly, filling the house with hideous laughter.

Undaunted, Wigglesworth commanded, "Be quiet. In the name of Jesus, come out of her, you foul spirits."

With a shriek and one last attempt to retain their grasp on the woman, thirty-seven different demonic spirits came out of her, giving their names as they exited. At the authority of the name of Jesus, the demons had to relinquish their territory, and the woman was totally delivered.

The fragile, exhausted wife was tenderly bathed and put to bed by a very grateful husband. She slept for fourteen hours while her family rejoiced at the power and love of a loving God.

The next morning, a beautiful young lady nursed her baby and then joined her parents, husband and Wigglesworth in a celebration of what the Lord had done. As they ate together, they gave thanks that the Lord had spared no expense to send His servant on such an errand of mercy.[1]

Endurance

Love gives faith supernatural ability and staying-power. Otherwise, our faith is in danger. The danger is the "clanging gong" or the "tinkling cymbal" syndrome. Paul described that kind of empty, insipid faith in his first letter to the Corinthians.

> *"Though I have all faith, so that I could remove mountains, but have not love* [or that "love anointing" on my faith], *I am nothing. And though I bestow all my goods to feed the poor, and though I give my body to be burned, but have not love, it profits me nothing."* (1 Corinthians 13:2–3)

The apostle is telling us that the gift or manifestation may look spectacular, but it will have no real, lasting benefit unless it is anointed by love, God's supernatural agape love. Have you ever seen that very thing? Have you been at a meeting where someone exhibited a special gift or two for awhile? There was a little flutter of excitement, a little response, but days or even hours later, nothing? People might say, "What was that? I don't even remember what was said?" Or, "It didn't last. What was happening there, anyway?" Well, it's quite likely the person was sincere. No doubt they had a measure of faith and they even manifested a genuine spiritual gift. But, it didn't have much love. Thus, it had no staying power. It had no lasting benefit. It was just a clanging gong, a tinkling cymbal.

Consider, then, another meeting and another manifestation of a spiritual gift like healing or prophecy. This time the person is moved by compassion. The love of God is energizing him or her. The healing or the prophecy comes forth. This time lives are changed forever. It bears wonderful fruit. The difference? Love. It is often not a question of faith but of love. Most of us have enough faith. Even a mustard seed sized portion will accomplish much. But are we walking in love?

Pitifully poor

The enemy can counterfeit a lot of things but his attempts at counterfeiting love are pitifully poor. That's why Paul says,

"Pursue love ... " Then he quickly adds, *" ... and desire spiritual gifts"* (1 Corinthians 14:1).

Jesus' faith was always anointed by love. In the gospel of Mark, we hear about the ruler. *"Jesus looked at* [the rich, young ruler] *and loved him"* (Mark 10:21 NIV). In the KJV, John calls it *"bowels of compassion"* (1 John 3:17).

Matthew says about Jesus, *"He saw a great multitude; and He was moved with compassion for them ... "* (Matthew 14:14). From compassion to action, again. Then what did He do? *" ... and healed their sick"* (verse 14 continued).

The time is now

Rick Warren, writing in *The Purpose Driven Life*, says,

> Sometimes procrastination is a legitimate response to a trivial task. But because love is what matters most, it takes top priority. The Bible stresses this repeatedly, saying:
>
> > *"Whenever we have the opportunity, we should do good to everyone."* (Galatians 6:10 NLT)
>
> > *"Use every chance you have for doing good."* (Ephesians 5:16 NCV)
>
> > *"Whenever you can, do good to those who need it. Never tell your neighbor to wait until tomorrow if you can help them now."* (Proverbs 3:27 TEV)

Why is now the best time to express love? Because you don't know how long you will have the opportunity. Circumstances change. People die. Children grow up. Tomorrow has few, if any, guarantees. If you want to express love, you had better do it now. Knowing that one day you will stand before God, here are some questions you need to consider: How will you explain those times when projects or things were more important to you than people? Who do you need to start spending more time with? What do you need to cut out of your schedule to make that possible? What sacrifices do you need to make? The best use of life is love. The best expression of love is time. The best time to love is now.[2]

Three quick tips

Here are three important and straight-forward things you can do to increase the "love anointing" in your own life and ministry:

1. ***Meditate on the cross***. Let's start there. The cross is where the old man dies and the new man (in Christ) is born (Galatians 2:20). John says, *"By this we know love, because He laid down His life for us"* (1 John 3:16). You and I will probably never ever fully comprehend the enormity of the price He paid for us. But, as we meditate on the cross of Christ something happens. An experience of the supernatural love of our Savior/Redeemer begins to rise up. Praise comes forth. Thanksgiving, too. And worship. You see what's happening? Self is decentralized. Self-consciousness, ego, personal pride and selfish ambition are dethroned. Jesus and His love becomes our focus and our very life.

2. ***Pray in the Spirit***. Jude 1:20 says, *"But you, beloved, building yourselves up on your most holy faith."* How do we build faith? It says, *"praying in the Holy Spirit"* (verse 20 continued). That's contrasted with praying with your mind. It means praying in tongues. Then it says, *"Keep yourself in the love of God."* Praying in the Spirit – a constant prayer flow of tongues, maintains a constant flow of love.

3. ***Press in***. Jesus' prayer of love in John 17:26 says, *"I have declared to them Your name, and I will declare it, that the love with which You loved Me may be in them, and I in them."* That's the same love! What was the quality of that love? Jesus was saying that the same passion, the same loyalty, the same affection, the same emotion, the same commitment, the same abandonment that the Father has for Jesus will be available to us. It will be there for all who will boldly press in for Jesus' love anointing.

And the winner is . . .

It is that very same love anointing that will radicalize our faith. It will bring forth an ability among all God's children to do the works of Jesus, healing the sick, casting out devils. We will even do the greater works that Jesus promised.

The Holy Spirit has anointed that verse of Scripture from John 17:26. In these last days He is brooding over the Church and He is bringing forth and birthing a holy desperation. Our Mighty God is bringing about an end-time, love-anointed, Bible-believing army that will absolutely plunder the ranks of hell to populate the forces of heaven. There will no longer be any "off limits" areas to Christians. No cease-fires. No time-outs. And all of the roaring, all of the snarls and threats, all of the deceptions and tricks and all the devices of Satan that have terrorized Christians for generations will be rendered null and void. He'll be done like dinner. Like badly burnt toast. There will be no safe place, and no safe time for this enemy. And the evil one will be powerless to stop it.

Might will make right. Count on it.

Notes

1. Hibbert, Albert, *Smith Wigglesworth: The Secret of His Power*, Tulsa, Harrison House, 1993, pp. 42–44.
2. Warren, Rick, *The Purpose Driven Life*, Grand Rapids, Zondervan.

Chapter 11

Five Amazing Words

I want to give you five words. These are common, ordinary words, easy to memorize and repeat. However, they are very powerful words. They can be life transforming! In fact, there is a guarantee that, if you use them properly, they will change your circumstances for the better! These words are: MAY-I-PRAY-FOR-YOU?

Did you know that most people in North America have never had anyone ask them that question? That most of the lost and suffering and dying souls around the world have never had anyone pray directly for them? Ever? Further, did you know that you have something that is absolutely unique to you and no one else on this planet? It's your contact group; your world. No one else has the exact same set of people that they meet each day, week, or whenever. This group of yours, however casual, random and incidental it might appear to be, is a gift from God to you. It is your mission field and this is where you are to use these five words.

People rarely refuse prayers, so your simple request can open hearts. The pizza delivery fellow you see every Sunday at half-time of the football match; your tenth-grade English teacher who you bump into occasionally at the grocery store; the old man down the hall in apartment 5. Good things will happen when you offer to pray for others and lives will be changed.

And it's not just the lives of the ones receiving prayer. It also changes those who step out and do the praying. I've seen it again and again. People who have never evangelized in their lives, people who have never led anyone to the Lord, suddenly they are praying with strangers. They are leading people to Christ.

People are receiving healing, miracles of finance, healing of relationships. Lives are changed.

These five simple words have, as I've applied them, certainly affected me. They've changed my life. I've seen people healed on airplanes, in malls, at the supermarket, on the streets. Friends; strangers; colleagues; casual acquaintances – saved, delivered and set free. Some of them have grown close to Sue and me, changed forever because my wife or I have dared to ask them that simple question, "May I pray for you?" What a question! What a concept! What an opportunity!

If you are willing to embark upon this glorious adventure and are willing to pop the question, here are a few hints to make you effective:

1. ***Follow the Holy Spirit.*** Expect Him to lead you to the people He wants you to pray for. Don't just approach people mechanically or indiscriminately. Prayer is not a battering-ram. Approach people with love, humility and compassion.
2. ***Follow the peace of Christ.*** Wait until you have peace before you approach people with this question. If you are anxious or worried, people pick up on that. Expect Christ's peace that passes all understanding. Anxiety, worry, fear ... all these undercut and dissipate the anointing. Peace, on the other hand, increases the anointing.
3. ***Have a servant attitude.*** Be genuinely interested in people and their problems/needs. Ask questions. Then, when they invite you to pray, pray the answers.
4. ***Make it short!***
5. ***Keep your eyes open.*** And, if you are in public, don't ask them to close their eyes.
6. ***Look for people with their heads down.*** In other words, look for people who have a need and know it. Look for people who don't appear arrogant, but rather, for those who are bowed by the problems of life. These are usually the ones who are very interested in Jesus and might want to come to church.
7. ***Let the love of Christ shine through you.***
8. ***And again, keep it short!***

Just last week Sue and I were buying a dishwasher. We were with two salesmen. One of the men, the chief salesman, was from Romania. The other man, a trainee, was from Cuba. We welcomed them both to Canada. We chit-chatted a bit, asked a bit about their backgrounds, then completed the purchase. After taking care of the business end of our visit, I said, "May I pray for you both?" The men both said, "Yes!" As I prayed brief prayers, the words became prophetic blessings. For the first man, I prayed financial blessing and that he would have the best sales day yet that very day. For the Cuban I also prayed prophetic words.

The other day, the Romanian man phoned me. Apparently, he and his friend were very much touched by the prayer. He told me, "You prayed for the best sales day yet. Do you know that that very day I made more money than I have ever made in my life? My sales were off the charts." Then he announced that he would come to church with me. The other man is also very interested in Jesus and wants to come to church, too!

So, be encouraged. You can do it, too. Remember the five words that will, I guarantee, change your life, if you aren't already using them: MAY-I-PRAY-FOR-YOU?

Appointment in Australia

As our healing team seeks to minister to those in need around the world, we are always looking for opportunities, such as the one with the dishwasher salesmen. We always look first to Jesus, and as we do, He gives us divine appointments. One such appointment in Australia resulted in signs and wonders in public places. The following is an account of our experiences there, by Dr. Knight of Sydney, Australia.

Into the marketplace
by Dr. Jenny Knight
From the very early stages of planning the time Bob Brasset and Gord Whyte would spend in Australia, our church's pastoral staff felt strongly that the time should be spent in ways other than conference presentations with their limited scope of structured lectures and tight schedules.

The church's intercessory prayer group spent much time in prayer seeking God's will in the direction to be taken. Gradually, a vision grew to use the time as an opportunity to take the gospel to the marketplace. Why limit the healing gifts to those able to attend a conference? Why not take those gifts to the marketplace? So it was that plans were made for Bob, Gord and Jan to visit the workplaces of three church members. One of these three was my husband, James, an HR manager with the state government's Department of Corrective Services. The other two were a medical practitioner, and a consultant with the Department of Housing, another government agency. A visit was also planned to an outreach ministry run by two church members.

As the conference drew closer and the three reported to the church on the progress they were making in preparing their workplaces for the visit, many of us realized (with no small amount of chagrin) how relieved we were that it was not us asked to host a healing and prayer session in our workplace. Not all had the amount of boldness required to take such a huge step of faith. That in itself was an important lesson for many.

James took the challenge in his stride. The process of obtaining permission from an intransigent bureaucracy took weeks and was in itself an act of faith. They had never before been asked to host a healing session! There was some opposition (advertising posters removed as soon as he put them up), but nothing directed at him personally.

As he looks back over the past few months he sees that there have been people placed in his path with whom he has had an opportunity to speak (and in some instances pray). These people were the first he asked to come along.

On the day of their first visit to James' work there was a degree of apprehension and doubt. Would anyone turn up? Would he be embarrassed in front of work colleagues, people he saw every day? What would Bob, Gord and Jan do and say? Looking back we can see that God must have had a chuckle over our lack of faith!

Bob, Gord and Jan were simply spectacular. The only word
we could use to describe their approach was "appropriate".
They were sensitive and caring. They won people over with
their compassion and interest (to say nothing of their
natural charm). Any initial awkwardness on the part of
those who came along quickly dissipated as they realized
these guys were genuine. Before we knew it, praying at work
seemed the most natural thing to do.

Early on in the session, Jan recounted a picture she
believed God had revealed to her on the journey into the
city. She saw an adult woman become a young girl and then
resume the look of an adult. The woman was clinging onto a
large pillar. She had asked God what the picture meant and
was told that a woman would be at the meeting who, as a
child, had been violently sexually abused. The name of the
pillar the woman was clinging to was "justice". Having told
her story, Jan then simply added, "I am here for you – if I
have come for no one else today I have come to pray with
you."

Totally unbeknownst to Jan, a young woman was present
who had been repeatedly sexually abused as a child. Her
abuser, a close family friend, had recently started abusing
her again. Her story, which out of sheer desperation and
fear, she had shared one day with James, was horrific. It
took a while but towards the end of the session she made
her way to Jan and made it known to her that she was
the woman/child in the picture God had given her that
morning. As a new Christian she was blown away by God's
provision.

The team visited James' workplace on two occasions. On
the second visit fewer people were present, many of them
making a return visit for a "top up". The session quickly
took on a very different tone as soon as Bob asked a group he
had been praying with if they would like to give their hearts
to the Lord. It was there in a government office in a tall
office tower in downtown Sydney that seven people bowed
their heads and asked Jesus to be their Savior. Those of us
from church were bowled over – it was all so simple!

Peculiar times, unexpected places

Sometimes we don't even have to ask. We just have to be ready to pray – at the most peculiar times and in the most unexpected places. My brother Edmund, who lives in Vancouver, has one such story. It all happened a few years back:

> Checking my wireless laptop screen I looked to find the first job assignment for the day. My employment was with a local telephone company, in installation and repair. Finding the business location, I noticed something different about this job. The door was locked and I had to press an intercom and request permission to enter. I did so and was "buzzed" in.
>
> The owner, Greg (not his real name), met me at the top of a long stairway and as I looked around I wondered what kind of place I was in. The reception room was large, with the usual desk and some cabinets on one side, but across from it was a dining room and a table with linens, dishes and cutlery. Huh? The company name on my laptop gave no hint as to the nature of the business since it was a numbered company. However, I was becoming quite curious as the owner led me from room to room or should I say, from bedroom to bedroom and finally to two offices at the end of the building.
>
> Greg explained what he wanted done in each room and I quickly estimated the time I would need. Two days, I told him. I started to work. First, I examined the old wiring and key splices. At one point I met some women in one of the offices. They were dressed in jeans and tee shirts. Later, as I was sorting through a maze of wires in the ceiling, I noticed the women had changed their clothes and were now wearing long, slinky dresses.
>
> "What's going on?" I thought to myself. Then it struck me – I was in a massage parlor! Suddenly I felt uncomfortable, but at almost the same instant the thought came to me, "Lord, You don't make mistakes."

An unusual deal

I climbed down from the ladder, and went down to talk to Greg in his office. I explained that I just realized where I was and that I was a born-again Christian. The only reason I was telling him this was that, although I felt uncomfortable, I knew that if I refused the job, the company would simply send someone else over to replace me immediately. The next words out of my mouth shocked me.

"I'll stay and complete the job," I told him, "if you come to church with me tonight."

Although it was Tuesday, our church was just finishing up a series of special meetings.

"Yes," Greg replied, much to my surprise. "Is it okay if I bring my daughter along, too?"

He then began telling me that his grandfather, the only person he loved when he was growing up, was a Christian, and had encouraged him to follow the Lord. He added that he had a brother in Alberta who was a Christian, as well, and who prayed for him daily.

An unusual request

Word got around the place, I guess, and later that afternoon the woman who was the office manager, came to me and asked if I would pray for the women. She explained that the job that they did was quite dangerous, and that they were sometimes beaten. All the women had children, as well. And many of the women, she told me, had suffered abuse growing up.

"What, specifically, would you like me to pray for?" I asked.

"Please pray that the Lord would protect all the women as they do their job."

I went with her down to her office where the women had gathered. She instructed someone to shut off all the telephones and asked them all to close their eyes and bow their heads because Ed was going to pray for them.

I prayed. I prayed that each woman there would come to know Jesus, and that He would protect them and their children. The presence of Jesus then enveloped us, right there, in that house of prostitution. I could feel the heart of Jesus for each and every woman. It was an amazing moment.

That evening my wife, our youngest daughter and I waited at the front of the church to see if Greg would come. And just before the service started he arrived, with his 11 year old daughter. Our daughter, Marie, took her and they went up and sat at the front with her friends. At the end of the service, his daughter responded to the altar call and gave her heart to Jesus. Greg was sitting with us and he was in tears.

"It doesn't matter what happens to me, now," he said, "because I know that my daughter is going to be with Jesus and she's going to see grandpa."

We asked him if he would like to commit his life to Jesus, as well. He responded that he would be a hypocrite because the money was very good in his business. He knew he was a pimp, he said, and he just couldn't let go of the money. So we asked him if there was any other thing that he would like us to pray about. He told us that he was going to have a meeting that night with someone who was trying to take over his business by threatening his daughter. My wife and I agreed to hold him in prayer. The next day I returned to work and all Greg could talk about was church the night before. He told all the women how his daughter became a Christian. He told me that the office manager was so impacted by my prayer and by the presence of Jesus the day before, that she had resigned her job.

Hugs and killings

I finally finished the job. A few days later Greg called me and asked me to come by and check the telephone programming. I asked him how the meeting with the other man had gone. He said that he prayed all the way to the meeting. When he first started out, he said, he thought that maybe he would have to kill the guy. But by the time he arrived, after all the prayer and everything, he didn't know what to do – hug him or kill him! He said he felt the love of Jesus for this man who was threatening the life of his daughter. And all he could see was a broken man. This other man then informed him he was leaving town and just wanted to borrow money for bus fare.

Greg was stunned. "Here," he told me over the phone, "was the man who hated me. And I knew that Jesus was real and that He was protecting me."

Greg and I stayed in contact. His daughter continued to accompany our daughter to youth group every Wednesday. Finally, though, we lost touch. Six months later I was working a Saturday afternoon. I was on my way home when I had the urge to take just one more job. Silly, I thought. I was done for the day. Yet I glanced at my laptop, anyway, and there were two jobs left. I picked one that seemed closest to my route home. As I neared the address I realized that it was the massage parlor again. "Lord, You don't make mistakes," I thought again.

Not the usual utterance

I hoped Greg would be there so I could talk to him about Jesus. But he wasn't. What a disappointment. So, instead, I got down to work. And as I was peering at splices and poking at connectors, the telephone rang. The office manager, a new woman, took the call. I asked her if it was Greg. She told me, yes. Could I speak with him, I asked her. She shrugged. Sure.

I took the receiver. "Hello, Greg. Are you coming to church with me tomorrow morning?"

Now I'm guessing that that's probably not the first thing a person would normally expect to hear when they call a house of prostitution. There was a long moment of complete silence, then finally a tentative, "Ed?" Then, "Yes. Yes. I'm coming. Ed, you wouldn't believe the miracles God is working in my life."

I laughed. "Oh yes I would!"

The next morning Greg arrived, with three women and a bodyguard. And at the end of the service he and his bodyguard went to the altar, knelt down, renounced their sins and accepted Jesus into their lives.

Chapter 12

Those Ancient Wells

Bobby Conner's prophecy in the mid-90s had and continues to have attention-grabbing authority and validity. In part, it said:

> I was then told that the coming volcanic activity near Bend, Oregon, would announce the beginning of one of the greatest healing revivals in history. This healing revival will start around Hamilton, Ontario and then blaze across Canada to Vancouver. From there, it will turn down the Northwest Coast of the U.S. and cross the Pacific to the Far East ... The Lord said that this local area in the Northwest was a seedbed of the healing anointing that was upon John G. Lake. The sign of volcanic activity around Bend, Oregon, is that the Lord is turning up the heat, but it will bring about a refining and purifying of His people so He can release healing in the earth in an unprecedented way.

I am convinced that this work is significant for the incipient healing revival that is upon us. We would do well to study the heritage of John G. Lake and to re-dig those ancient wells of faith and anointed believing. Not that we want to focus on a man or dwell on what happened in the past, but rather investigate historical God-given examples that can help us today. God has always worked through men and women who have pioneered and shown the way. It seems that there are things in the Spirit that can be inherited. If we will be faithful in a little, I believe God will, one day, take us beyond even what John G. Lake, Aimee Semple MacPherson, Kathryn Kuhlman, Charles Price,

John Wimber and others experienced. We thank God for these wonderful pioneers who went before and blazed a mighty trail of faith and courage.

Radical obedience

Several things stand out in the life of John G. Lake that point to the reason for his incredible power and authority. Among these things are his attitude towards wealth, his consecration and his willingness to die for the faith he held so dear. In these things, he stands in stark contrast with much of what today's Church emphasizes.

Dr. Ward M. Tannenberg, in his biography on the life of John G. Lake tells of how in his early years, Lake possessed an ability to accumulate wealth, and how Lake, when he knew he was called into the ministry, freely and gladly gave up this wealth:

> The first day he opened his office, he made $2,500.00 on a real estate deal. At the end of the twenty-one months, he had over $100,000.00 in the bank, a $30,000 paid-up life insurance policy and real estate valued at $90,000.00.
>
> His wealth increased from there but when he knew he was called into the ministry he gave all his worldly possessions away. In April, 1907, he closed his office door for the last time and disposed of his bank account by giving to various religious and educational institutions. Fred R. Burr, of Winamac, Indiana, who was his financial agent, assisted him in disposing of everything, including his real estate holdings.

Lake then led a life of walking by faith for all his financial needs along the lines of George Muller. Does that mean that in order to have a healing anointing, we too must give up all our finances and live by faith? Maybe or maybe not. I think the example and lesson for us from Lake's life is to emulate his radical obedience for the sake of the gospel. What is God calling you to do?

In the ninth chapter of Acts, Paul was assured by God, through Ananias, that his life would *not* be one of ease, but it *would* be one of power. God spoke to Ananias, "[Saul of Tarsus] *a chosen vessel of Mine to bear My name before Gentiles, kings, and the children of Israel. For I will show him how many thing he must suffer for My name's sake"* (Acts 9:15–16).

That is the message Jesus Christ, the crucified, resurrected and glorified Son of God, gave to the apostle Paul. He was not to live a life of holy ease: early retirement, golf vacations, his own line of designer togas, and Egypt Express Gold card. Instead, this apostle was destined for a desperate daily struggle and an incredible series of experiences brought him time and again to the brink of death. But he was destined, too, to see the dead raised, the sick healed and a multitude of captives set free. He would, in the end, pay the ultimate price for God's glory, power and anointing resting on him.

Paul himself recounts several incidents in his second letter to the city of Corinth:

> *"From the Jews five times I received forty stripes minus one. Three times I was beaten with rods; once I was stoned; three times I was shipwrecked; a night and a day I have been in the deep; in journeys often, in perils of waters, in perils of robbers, in perils of my own countrymen, in perils of the Gentiles, in perils in the city, in perils in the wilderness, in perils in the sea, in perils among false brethren; in weariness and toil, in sleeplessness often, in hunger and thirst, in fastings often, in cold and nakedness . . ."*
>
> (2 Corinthians 11:24–27)

When Paul speaks of receiving 39 lashes, he would have been stripped, whipped viciously with scourges, his flesh lacerated, bleeding and torn before falling into an unconscious stupor. Then he would have been doused with a bucket of salt water to keep the maggots away and dropped into a cold, damp dungeon. That, was the price of his apostleship. That was the price of Paul's healing and preaching anointing. But of all this God said he would, *". . . bear My name before Gentiles, kings, and the children of Israel"* (Acts 9:15). Was it worth it? To be an instrument of the Most High God? Ask him, when you see him. I wonder what he'll say?

Consecration

There is a depth of *consecration* revealed in Paul's words that is often lacking in our modern world. But God hasn't been idle. He is turning up the pressure and restoring this consecration to His body in these latter days. John G. Lake, in a 1908 sermon, described a desperate situation:

Do you want to know why God poured out His Spirit in South Africa like He did nowhere else in the world? There was a reason. The following example will illustrate. We had 125 men out on the field at one time. Our finances got so low we could not even mail to these workers, at the end of the month, a ten dollar bill. The situation was desperate. What was I to do? Under these circumstances, I did not want to take the responsibility of leaving men, and their families, on the frontier without real knowledge of what their conditions were.

Some of us at headquarters sold our clothing, certain pieces of furniture, anything we could, to bring these 125 workers off the field for a conference ...

One night in the conference, I was invited to leave the room for a minute or two.

When I came in, I found they had rearranged the chairs and had placed on a small table, at one end, the bread and the wine.

Old Father Van Der Wall, speaking for the company, said, "Brother Lake, during your absence, we have come to a conclusion. We have made our decision. We want to serve the Lord's Supper. We are going back to our fields. We are going back if we have to walk back. We are going back if we have to starve. We are going back if we, our wives, and our children face death. If we have to die, we have but one request ... if we die, we want you to come and bury us."

Jesus Christ put the spirit of martyrdom in the ministry. Jesus instituted His ministry with a pledge unto death ... on the last night He took the cup, when He drank, saying,

"Beloved, this cup is the New Testament in my blood." Then He said, "Drink all of it."

Friends, the group of missionaries that followed me went without food and went without clothes. This is the kind of consecration that established Pentecost in South Africa.

Historians declare that the blood of the martyrs is the seed of the Church. Could it be that a difficulty in our day is that we have so little seed in the Western Church? In China they have much seed and they have much power. The Western Church needs more martyr blood.

Lake declared, "If I were pledging men and women to the Gospel of the Son of God as I am endeavoring to do tonight, it would not be to have a nice church and harmonious surroundings and a sweet do-nothing time. I would invite them to be ready to die."

That was the spirit of early Methodism. John Wesley established a heroic call. He demanded of every preacher to *be ready to pray, ready to preach and ready to die.*

That is always the spirit of Christianity. When any other spirit comes into the Church, it is not the spirit of Christianity. It is a foreign spirit. Lake described the ongoing attitude, "The reason we never had splits in our work in South Africa ... [is] ... men who are ready to die for the Son of God do not split. They do not complain the first time they get hunger pangs."

David Hogan in Mexico walks in an amazing anointing. He and his team do a total fast every second day, plus they do other fasts throughout the year as the Lord directs. They have raised 200 people from the dead as a result of this ministry. What is the secret of their power? Hogan says it's that their lives [Hogan's team] are not their own. They have been bought with a price. It is their consecration unto death.

In his tape series on his ministry, David Hogan talks about how he doesn't even like to leave Mexico for the rest of North America (the U.S. and Canada). Why not? It's because of what he perceives to be our luke-warmness, our compromise, and our unwillingness to lay down our lives, to lay it all down on the altar.

It's about freedom

Because of what Jesus did on the cross, you and I now have freedom. Paul said, *"We preach Christ crucified"* (1 Corinthians 1:23). Why preach that? Because it is our power source. Paul was pretty explicit, it is: *"the power of God"* (verse 24). If you want power and authority to heal the sick, preach the cross. But start by living it! The cross brings us freedom. It's a glorious freedom. It's also death! A death sentence to the old way of life.

The Lord has blessed me tremendously but He still requires that I be willing to die. And each and every day I have to face that choice anew. To follow Jesus to the cross, die, and live forever. Or to save my life and lose it all, terribly, in the end. The apostle Paul said, *"I die daily"* (1 Corinthians 15:31). Theologians some-times over-spiritualize that declaration. They interpret it to mean, "I die to *self* daily." But let's not muddle the facts. The context is quite clear. Paul wasn't just denying himself a cigarette and a quick nine holes on the golf course. He was facing the very real threat, every time he opened his mouth to speak, of beatings, imprisonment and death. He faced it and he went through it.

Dutch Sheets said, "The cross is not something you wear around your neck. It's supposed to wear you."

"If anyone desires to come after me," Jesus admonished, *"let him deny himself, and take up his cross, and follow Me"* (Matthew 16:24).

Jesus further said, *"You will receive power when the Holy Spirit has come upon you; and you shall be witnesses to Me"* (Acts 1:8). The Greek word for witness, remember, is *martyrus*. Another trans-lation of that word is "living evidence". So we are called to be living, walking, breathing evidence that Jesus is alive. And we are to be willing to lay down our lives if the call comes.

Bobby Conner prophesied that the Lord is "turning up the heat". Why? Because it will bring about a refining and a purifying of His people, so that He can release healing in the earth in an unprecedented way. My encouragement to all is this: Let's submit to the refining and the purifying. Let's take this glorious anointing for healing to the ends of the earth. Let's consider the life of John G. Lake, look to his example for that seedbed of unshakeable faith and the healing anointing that was upon his life.

Sleepless in Spokane

My wife Sue and I were scheduled to go to Spokane, Washington on April 17th and 18th, 2003. Spokane, as many of you know, is the city where John G. Lake ministered with powerful healing miracles for many years. During his years of ministry there were 100,000 documented healings! As a result, some members of the medical profession called Spokane the healthiest city in America. Prior to our coming, several pastors and congregations had been interceding, fasting, praying late into the night and calling out to God: "Do it again, Lord. Revisit Spokane with Your glorious healing power."

As we walked along the tarmac to board the plane I looked at Sue. She was suddenly glowing with gold dust. Her hands and her face sparkled with a fine metallic substance. Then God spoke to my heart, "I am about to visit these upcoming meetings with my glory." He did not disappoint!

That first night a standing-room only congregation saw amazing demonstrations of His glory. As I stood to speak, people had already begun to experience healings. It sure wasn't me doing it. Some had even been healed on the way to the meeting. Gold dust, gold fillings, and silver fillings were appearing all over the auditorium. Then, after words of knowledge, there were more healings. And after the message, still more healings! Then there were salvations. Then more miracles and healings, testimonies and gold dental miracles. Even an infant in the nursery had gold dust on it. Does that sound like it was starting to be old hat? Not to those being healed, it wasn't.

We called all the pastors forward from all the churches and congregations represented at the meeting. And as they stood, Sue and I prayed a transfer of the healing/miracle anointing. The result? Monday morning the phone calls began coming in. One pastor shared, "I couldn't preach. Healings and testimonies took up the whole service!"

Then our services on Sunday were more of the same: praise; worship; intercession; more praise! Then, from the pulpit a word of exhortation, during which, I think I can safely say, nobody slept!

Walking and leaping

Healings flowed in great abundance, both before and after the word in Spokane. Screams and shouts erupted from different parts of the congregation as more gold teeth were manifested. One daughter touched her mother's new gold tooth, then jumped back in shock. It was, she said later, hot to touch, and electricity raced up and down her hand and arm as she touched it.

One man with multiple sclerosis was sitting in his wheelchair and he received a new gold tooth. Three minutes later, as people watched, he received another one!

A woman had arthritis and very poor vision. She was healed of both problems.

Another woman was unable to walk unaided. The power of God hit her. She got up and walked naturally and easily.

One woman reported being healed of cancer. Then five gold teeth appeared in her mouth. She began to dance.

Deaf ears were opened up.

Lumps and tumors were dissolved.

One of the most thrilling healings for me, personally, was that of a father and daughter. I asked for a show of hands for all those with pain in their bodies. This man and girl both raised theirs. I called them forward to demonstrate how easily God heals people. This father had an incurable condition in the arms and hands that had caused great discomfort and suffering, for about three years if I remember correctly. His daughter, seven or eight years old, was in tears with stomach pain. They stood together on the platform as the congregation extended their hands. The power of God hit them both. Within moments they were both healed.

Sue and I will never forget the incredible love and kindness from the pastors and people of Spokane. We will long remember the awesome healing anointing. It seemed nothing was imposs-ible. No disease, no infirmity, no sickness stood before the mighty authority of the Lord Jesus Christ. It was truly an explosion of God's healing love.

Passionate faith

"And shall God not avenge His own elect who cry out day and night to Him, though He bears long with them?"   (Luke 18:7)

It is my conviction that the only kind of faith that has any joy in it or any lasting power is *passionate* faith. Jesus was passionate with desire towards His Father. He was passionate in doing His will.

Children know how to be passionate. Sometimes their un-adulterated enthusiasm "catches" their parents off-guard. In fact, when my children were growing up, if I ever said anything that even remotely smacked of a promise it was set in stone, cast in bronze and written into the law of the land. They really, really held me to my word. If, for example, they requested a trip to the movies the following weekend, my answer might have been, "Possibly, if I have time off, am well-rested, and am not too busy." To them that was an emphatic "Yes!" Great! So, come next Saturday, even if I was completely exhausted and up to my eyebrows in work with not a moment to spare, there they would be at the front door, whooping, hopping up and down, ready to leave for the movies. They had childlike passion and a childlike understanding of what faith is. They took me at my word – at least what they understood of it. Our Heavenly Father wants us to have that same childlike attitude towards Him.

Desperate desire

Someone once said, "I've never had a desperate prayer go unanswered." What happens in a crisis? We pray with passion. God sees the desperation, the passion, and the intensity of our prayer and He delights to respond. Then, when our crisis is over, we return to mediocrity. God isn't pleased.

A friend of mine, a former U.S. Senator, once had a vision. A modern day prophet had prophesied to him that he and his wife would have a son, and they would name him Caleb, and that Caleb would do great exploits in the name of the Lord. Before any of that could happen, however, the Senator needed to have an operation. During the operation his heart stopped beating and he died. But his wife didn't accept his death. She laid hold of his feet. She prayed and interceded, saying in essence, "No, you shall not die. We are to have a son, and we are to name him Caleb, and he will do great exploits in the name of the Lord. The Lord has promised us!"

He came back to life! And he said later that during the time that he was clinically dead, with no vital signs, he was in the presence of the Lord, and he had the following vision: The Lord showed him seven mountains with names like education, arts and entertainment, finance, etc., on the top of each of the mountains. Then he saw an eighth mountain grow and become much larger than the others, reaching up to the heavens. This eighth mountain, the Lord told him, represented the Kingdom of God. The middle of this mountain, at the same height as the peaks of the other mountains, represented mediocrity. While the peak of this mountain of the Kingdom of God represented excellence and strong desire.

> *"I know your works, that you are neither cold nor hot ... I will vomit you out of My mouth."*   (Revelation 3:15–16)

Chapter 13

Faith Times Four

Some Bible teachers have implied that the only way to get healed is to personally reach out and "get faith", and by a simple act of faith, appropriate your healing. The implication is that, somehow, we must *develop* (usually by reading Scripture) enough personal faith and then step out and exercise that faith. This personal faith, in turn, obtains our healing. I suggest that this teaching is inadequate and incomplete. I propose other dimensions to faith that some teachers have overlooked. What follows is a listing of four different dimensions of the exercise of faith.

1. *Seeking faith.* This is the faith that we see, on occasion, in the gospels when people actively seek out their own healing. Matthew 9:27–30 reads,

   "When Jesus departed from there, two blind men followed Him, crying out and saying, 'Son of David, have mercy on us!' And when He had come into the house, the blind men came to Him. And Jesus said to them, 'Do you believe that I am able to do this?' They said to Him, 'Yes, Lord.' Then He touched their eyes, saying, 'According to your faith, let it be to you.' And their eyes were opened."

   Wouldn't it be great, then, if we could make a formula out of this? If, when we meet every blind person, we could say, "Do you believe that I, by the grace and power of God, am able this very instant to heal your eyes?"

Or would it even work? Note carefully what Jesus said, "According to your faith, be it done unto you." Jesus, on this particular occasion, put the focus directly on their own faith. I call this seeking faith. This was the active ingredient, the trigger mechanism.

In this same chapter in Matthew, we see another outstanding example of seeking faith. Matthew 9:20–22 (NIV) says,

> *"Just then a woman who had been subject to bleeding for twelve years came up behind him and touched the edge of his cloak. She said to herself, 'If I only touch his cloak, I will be healed.' Jesus turned and saw her. 'Take heart, daughter,' he said, 'your faith has healed you.' And the woman was healed from that moment."*

2. **Intercessory faith.** Intercessory faith is faith exercised on behalf of someone else who is ill and needs healing. Mark 5:21–24 (NIV) tells us,

> *"When Jesus had again crossed over by boat to the other side of the lake, a large crowd gathered round him while he was by the lake. Then one of the synagogue rulers, named Jairus, came there. Seeing Jesus, he fell at his feet and pleaded earnestly with him, 'My little daughter is dying. Please come and put your hands on her so that she will be healed and live.' So Jesus went with him. A large crowd followed and pressed around him."*

Then Jesus was interrupted by a request for another healing. He performed this healing and as a result was delayed. Then a messenger came to Jairus with the dreadful news, "Your daughter has died. Why trouble the teacher any more?" Jesus overheard the comment and said to the synagogue official, "Do not be afraid any longer. Only believe."

Jesus went to Jairus' house and allowed no one to follow with Him except Peter, James and John. There was a great commotion around the house with people weeping and wailing, but Jesus only said, "Why make a commotion and weep? The child has not died but is asleep!"

Further, the Bible says, "And they began laughing at Him. And putting them all out, He took along the child's father and mother and His own companions. Entering the room where the child was, and taking the child by the hand, He said to her, 'Talitha Kum' (which translated means, little girl, I say to you arise!) and immediately the little girl arose and began to walk."

There was faith at work here. The father had enough faith to ask Jesus in the first place, even though she was on the point of death. He also had enough faith to stick with Jesus, even after she was dead and the people were laughing and making fun of Jesus. The problem was that the people surrounding them had no understanding whatever of the possibility of these things happening, even with Jesus!

My apprehension and misgiving is that, in the Church today, we are not unlike those people around Jairus' house that day. We have very little understanding of the mercy and compassion of Jesus in this realm.

Another instance of intercessory faith is in Luke 5:18–26. On this occasion, four friends brought a paralyzed man to Jesus. It says here, *"When He [Jesus] saw their faith"* He healed the man. There it is again – intercessory faith. Jesus didn't ask for or expect the paralyzed man to exercise faith. The significant component was the faith of the four friends and this is recorded in the three synoptic gospels.

3. *Ministry faith*. The next type of faith for healing in the Gospels is ministry faith. Acts 3 records a very good example in verses 1–11 (NIV). It's the healing at the gate called Beautiful. You'll remember that Peter and John were going up to pray at the temple. They encountered a beggar asking for alms.

"Peter looked straight at him, as did John. Then Peter said, 'Look at us!' So the man gave them his attention, expecting to get something from them. The Peter said, 'Silver or gold I do not have, but what I have I give you. In the name of Jesus Christ of Nazareth, walk.' Taking him by the right hand, he helped him up, and instantly the man's feet and ankles became strong. He

jumped to his feet and began to walk. Then he went with them into the temple courts, walking and jumping, and praising God. When all the people saw him walking and praising God, they recognized him as the same man who used to sit begging at the temple gate called Beautiful, and they were filled with wonder and amazement at what had happened to him."

(verses 4–10)

Whose faith got the lame man to his feet? Peter addressed the man. Peter lifted the man. Peter invoked the name of Jesus. It wasn't the lame man's faith. He didn't claim his healing. He didn't struggle.

Acts 3:16 says, *"By faith in the name of Jesus, this man whom you see and know was made strong."* It was the faith of Peter, and the power associated with "the name". This is ministry faith and we see it again and again in Scripture.

4. ***Corporate or combined faith***. This involves a group or a team of people operating together. We see a clear example in James 5:14–15,

"Is anyone among you sick? Let him call for the elders of the church, and let them pray over him, anointing him with oil in the name of the Lord. And the prayer of faith [team prayer] *will save* [or heal] *the sick and the Lord will raise him up."*

There are three parts to this word. First comes the healing, secondly the raising up, and lastly, if he has committed sins, they shall be forgiven. In verse 16 (NIV) it tells us, *"Confess your sins one each other . . . that you may be healed."* Abraham is the example. Abimelech's family was unable to bear children. Abraham prayed for them (Genesis 20:17–18) and they were healed. And in the next two verses, Sarah, Abraham's wife, also conceived and bore a child (Genesis 21:1–2). The effective, fervent prayer of a righteous person avails much (James 5:16). It's interesting. Sickness, it appears, should be an unlikely or uncommon occurrence in the Church. Jesus doesn't say *when* you sin . . . he says *if* you sin. Look it up. It's all over the place in Scripture. *If* you sin.

In Acts 14:19–20, Paul had just been stoned and left for dead. As the disciples stood round about him, he rose up and came into the city. It was not Paul's faith that raised him up from death or near death. He was actually left for dead. This means that those who stoned him were convinced that either he was dead or death was imminent. Still, the disciples who were, it says, "gathered about him", quite probably prayed and earnestly interceded. God answered their prayers. Their faith on Paul's behalf enabled Paul to be raised up and to continue his ministry.

A place of rest

Anointed believing is a place. It's a position in Christ. And this position in Christ is a place of rest. In fact, Jesus invites all weary people to come to Him and rest. He says, *"Take my yoke upon you and learn from me, for I am gentle and humble in heart, and you will find rest for your souls"* (Matthew 11:29 NIV). Simple anointed faith will bring us to rest. *"For we who have believed do enter that rest"* (Hebrews 4:3).

Habakkuk 2:20 is an example of rest: *"But the Lord is in His holy temple. Let all the earth keep silence before Him."* The margin of my NASB reads this way, "Hush before Him, all the earth." This idea of being caught up in His tranquil quietness is found also in Psalm 23:2, *"He leads me beside the still waters [or waters of rest]."* Psalm 46:10 reads, *"Be still, and know that I am God; I will be exalted among the nations, I will be exalted in the earth!"* The margin of my NASB also reads uniquely, "Let go, relax!" Many of us are trained to be so busy *doing something* for the Kingdom of God! The thought of relaxing and letting go is altogether a new prayer discipline – one we all can really enjoy!

Bull's eye

The apostle Paul tells us, *". . . you stand by faith"* (Romans 11:20). Faith, or trusting God, is the simplest condition God could have required.

Faith in the Bible is never separated from the object of faith. Jesus did not say to His disciples, "Have faith". More specifically, He said, *"Have faith in God"* (Mark 11:22). The God who created the universe and sustains it all by His own Word, is He not completely worthy of our fullest confidence?

John G. Patten is the man who first translated the Bible into the language of the New Hebrides. He had a problem. He couldn't find a word in that language that represented faith or believing. One day, a native workman he had hired came into the hut and, lying back on the couch, said in his own tongue, "Oh, I am so tired, I am going to rest my whole weight on this couch."

That's it! thought Patten. I have my word!

"God so loved the world that He gave His only begotten son, that whosoever rests his whole weight upon Him should not perish, but have everlasting life" (John 3:16).

A continuum of confidence

Faith is simply resting our whole weight in the arms of our faithful Father. He declared, *"The just shall live by faith"* (Galatians 3:11). You believed, rested on Him yesterday. Continue to believe and rest today. And then believe and rest on Him tomorrow. It is a continuous flow, a continuum of confidence. As you keep looking unto Jesus, the author and perfecter (or finisher) of your faith, you will find something exciting. You will find the exercise of faith as simple as breathing. There'll come a continuous inflow and outflow of His life and His Spirit.

This is why the writer to the Hebrews tells us, *"For we have become partakers of Christ if we hold the beginning of our confidence steadfast to the end"* (Hebrews 3:14). Yesterday's faith won't do for today. It really won't. Today we must draw anew, trust anew and rest anew in Him. And as we do, something absolutely wonderful and altogether supernatural happens! We are changed. We are transformed; we are metamorphosed – to transliterate a Greek word – from one measure of glory, to another, and yet another. *"Do not be conformed to this world, but be transformed [metamorphoso in Greek] by the renewing of your mind"* (Romans 12:2).

Responding to promises

There is a wonderful promise in 2 Corinthians 1:19:

> *"For the Son of God, Jesus Christ, who was preached among you by us – by me, Silvanus, and Timothy – was not Yes and No, but in Him was Yes."*

This means God's Word is not uncertain or unstable. It always says the same thing. It is always true. For example, God's Word does not indicate that sometimes healing is available and sometimes it is not. What does it say? The NIV version renders verse 20 like this:

> *"For no matter how many promises God has made, they are 'Yes' in Christ. And so through him the 'Amen' is spoken by us to the glory of God."*

Note that when Paul says this, the New Testament had not yet been compiled. He's saying all the promises such as:

> *"I am the LORD who heals you."*   (Exodus 15:26)

> *"I will take sickness away from the midst of you."*
>   (Exodus 23:25)

> *"Nor shall any plague come near your dwelling."*
>   (Psalm 91:10)

These are all promises and Paul says, *"For all the promises of God in Him are Yes, and in Him Amen, to the glory of God through us"* (2 Corinthians 1:20). All those tremendous Old Testament promises, the covenantal promises, are "yes" and "so be it". There is, therefore,

- No hesitating
- No uncertainty
- No works required
- No doubting

Again, all those promises are "yes" and "so be it". When we are good, when we are bad, even when we are indifferent, straddling the fence, so to speak, God still holds out His merciful healing hand to those of us who will exercise faith (or trust) and will dare to believe God.

Let us not cast away our confidence for we are assured it will have great recompense or reward. The saintly Andrew Murray has given us some simple rules for a life of continuous, anointed believing and unbroken communion with God:

1. *Take time to meet God.*
2. *Take time until you know God is very near.* *"Draw near to God and He will draw near to you"* (James 4:8).
3. *Take time to humble yourself before God.* Be silent before God and let Him bless you.

Authentic and humble

Jim Goll had a vision a few years back. In it he saw a boxing ring. Two pugilists emerged from opposite corners with red gloves. The contestants engaged each other and a bloody battle ensued. Then the bell rang and a voice spoke, "It's time for humble, authentic faith to enter the ring."

I believe we are in that time frame. There has been a battle and at times it has been bloody. The battle is over our faith expression and over what kind of faith is genuine and authentic. It's a battle to manifest true, God-honoring faith. There have been, over the past three decades, expressions of faith in the Church that have been arrogant and disingenuous. It's time for the real thing, for humble authentic faith to emerge. When it does, we will do the very works of Jesus and then the greater works (John 14:12). We will go from sporadic healing to the point where the grace of God will unblock creative miracles.

Jim Goll said that three things need to come together in a meeting for great healing and miracles to happen:

1. Attitude of special faith.
2. The manifest presence of God.
3. The presence of releasers/imparters.

It is like the three-stranded cord that is not easily broken (Ecclesiastes 4:12). If only one strand such as "special faith" is present, then some healing takes place. If two strands are present, we have more demonstration of God's power. If all three are there, then much happens.

Here come the champions

The apostolic and the prophetic is being restored in our generation. These are the releasers and the imparters. They will emerge in two ways:

1. *As a nameless-faceless generation.* That is, they won't attempt to make a name for themselves or to build their own reputations. In this they will remain nameless and faceless.
2. *As dread champions.* They will be dreaded – by the enemy, that is! Their names will be known in hell, but written in heaven. They will pioneer to open up areas and regions. They will be overcomers to break demonic oppression. They will be prophetic imparters and apostolic releasers.

But woe to the superstars

An emphasis on power, on miracles and on healing without a corresponding emphasis on character always leads to sensationalism and ultimately, a decrease in power. Like the church at Sardis, the presence and favor of the Holy Spirit will die while the church continues to, or attempts to live on, the reputation of past glories. Remember how it went with Sampson, mightiest man of all the earth. When he was captured by his enemies his initial reaction was scorn. *"I will go out as before, at other times, and shake myself free. But he did not know that the* Lord *had departed from him"* (Judges 16:20).

Dutch Sheets in his book, *The River of God*, writes concerning this Samson effect,

> This pattern inevitably leads to cynicism on the part of the world and disillusionism in the church. I have watched

several churches and ministries built this way. Excitement prevailed, Christians transferred and these works become the latest, fastest growing, cutting-edge overnight sensation. The magazines came. Articles were written. TV shows were produced and money was made. Many of them are now dead or mortally wounded. Others still have a name. They're alive, but are basically dead. Heaven weeps while we go do it somewhere else, creating another overnight sensation, playing our kingdom success games.[1]

Genuine greatness

When it really counts, standing before the throne of the Almighty One at the end of time, who among us are going to be the true superstars? Okay, so superstar is a corrupted and misapplied word. Instead, then, I would ask who you think are the really great people? We are not considering the size of a person's congregation, or counting the number of people who fall to the floor when they lay hands on them, or the number of people who are anxious to count them as a close, personal friend.

Of course you knew that, didn't you? We just tend to forget it occasionally. We must remind ourselves and be reminded over and over that, despite all the Christian flash, Christian glitz, and "showy" evidence to the contrary, true greatness is found elsewhere.

It's not that gifting of itself is bad, or wrong. Absolutely not. When applied correctly, it's a tool of God. But it's not His heart. The heart of God, the very essence of God of which the angels around His throne boast continuously, is His character. And how we mortals on earth reflect that character is what truly matters. Everything else then, every gift, every blessing, every good thing, is but a means to that end.

In conclusion

Finally, let me point out this fact: All of Scripture, all of prophecy, all of revelation point to this one fact. In these concluding moments of time God is about to give a revelation of the most glorious thing this world has ever seen. God is about to give the world a full-on revelation of His Son's glorious bride and her magnificent bridegroom. An anointed, believing army of end-time bondservants who will plunder hell and populate heaven. And He says to His bride, *"Arise, shine; for your light has come! And the glory of the LORD is risen upon you"* (Isaiah 60:1).

Note

1. Sheets, Dutch, *The River of God*, Ventura, Gospel Light.

About the Author

Bob Brasset, an international speaker and teacher, is known for his ministry of healing. His home is Victoria, B.C., Canada, where his Extreme Healing Ministry is based and where he now fills the position of team leader and co-coordinator.

Bob attended St. Francis Xavier University in Nova Scotia and St. Francis Seminary in Milwaukee, Wisconsin. He then pastored churches on Vancouver Island for about 20 years. In 1998, while on a trip to Norwich, Connecticut, Bob was visited with a special anointing in the area of healing and the miraculous. Upon his return to Victoria and his home church, Bob found the healing anointing was released quite unexpectedly and powerfully. Soon invitations were coming in from many parts of the world. Bob responded and he now travels extensively throughout the nations, training, releasing, equipping and holding healing/ evangelistic campaigns.

Experience as an artist, husband, father and pastor/teacher has given Bob a rich, blended ministry of God's grace, miraculous healing power, and deliverance. He places special emphasis on what he calls the "love anointing" – that is, the compassion of the Father heart of God for the hurting, the broken, the sick and the oppressed.

Since January, 1998, Bob and his wife Sue have poured themselves out in releasing God's healing power and authority to many cities and nations.

Contact information for Bob Brasset:

129 Granada Crescent,
Victoria, BC, V8B 2B8

Email: rsbrasset@shaw.ca
Website: www.extremehealing.ca